CW01023242

# The Register of Death

## A History of Executions at Walton Prison, Liverpool

### John Smith

First Published 2007

Published by Countyvise.

Copyright © 2007 John Smith

The right of John Smith to be identified as the author of this work has been asserted by him in accordance with the Copyright, Design and Patents Act 1988.

British Library Cataloguing in Publication Data.

A catalogue record for this book is available from the British Library.

ISBN 978-1901-231-92-2

# Acknowledgements

I would like to express my thanks to the following people who helped to make the writing of this book possible.
William Shearer, who shared his great knowledge of the history of Liverpool Prison with me. Jeff Swindells who put himself out, time and time again to assist me with my research. My friends Jimmy Bainbridge and Peter Williams who were always on hand to read, and correct any mistakes in the stories. Steve Jones, Librarian at Liverpool Prison for his advice and support. My good friend Sally Lynam for proof reading the original stories. Liverpool Record Office and staff for their great help and assistance in the research of the book.

My colleague's Alan Tottey, John Mooney, Bob McLean and Ray Banks who have gone out of their way, to point out that I wouldn't have had time to write the book, if they hadn't done my work.

My special thanks to Julia Cuerdon and Roberta Cuerdon Jones for their great support.

# The Register of Death
## Introduction to Walton Prison

In 1847 after years of consultation between Liverpool Corporation and the Home Office, an agreement was finally reached to build a new prison in Liverpool.

Liverpool Corporation purchased land in Walton for £228 per acre. The construction of the prison was at Hornby Road, Liverpool and was carried out by Furness & Co, the Architect was John Weightman Esq. The building was completed in 1855.

The reason for the building of this new prison, was to replace the older New Borough Gaol, Great Howard Street, Liverpool some three miles away. This overcrowded prison which had been opened in 1795 and housed French prisoners of war, was known as the "French Gaol". It would close its door within weeks of Walton Prison opening. The building was demolished the same year, the prisoners were transferred to Walton prison.

Walton Prison was the second prison in Liverpool, the other prison being Kirkdale Gaol some two miles away. This prison had been built in 1819 and would close in 1892.

The site at Hornby Road, covered some fifteen acres, and would in 1980 be extended to twenty two acres.

At the time of completion, the new prison which took the name Walton Gaol, was the most modern prison in Europe. It provided single cell accommodation with basic integral sanitation, for inmates in eleven wings.

Now some 150 years later it has become the largest prison in Europe, able to accommodate nearly 1400 inmates whose sentences cover crimes, from motoring offences to murder.

When the prison was first opened, it could hold up to 1,000 inmates. Both male and female inmates occupied the wings, this continued to be the case until 1933, when female inmates were moved to other prisons, leaving Walton Gaol receiving male prisoners only.

The regime at the prison was a harsh one, intending that serving a sentence at the prison would deter inmates from returning. Inmates were given tough uncompromising hard labour at the tread wheel, pumping the day's water supply from the ground to water tanks in the roof space. The silent system was introduced, the only sound was the ticking of the tower clock.

The idea of using a tread wheel at Walton Prison, was copied from the much older Kirkdale Gaol, which had the largest tread wheel in the country

During the second World War, the prison suffered serious damage from enemy action. In May, 1941, there were raids on successive nights, the prison received eight direct hits killing 22 inmates, and demolishing entirely, C and D wings.

Capital punishment was the order of the day for offences of murder, but executions continued to be carried out at Kirkdale Gaol, until Monday, 13th March, 1887 when the first execution took place at Walton Gaol.

Over the next 77 years, a total of 62 executions would take place at the prison, which would throughout the country be known as "Walton Jail" .

The last execution would take place on 13th August, 1964.

The executed prisoners would be buried within the walls of the prison, sometimes, two or three executed prisoners would be buried in the same grave.

Details of these executions are kept in a book, known as the Death Register, or Register of Death. This book is kept in a safe in the works department at the prison.

This book is one of the oldest documents still kept at the prison. It contains details of the deceased person, date of execution, number of the grave, and burial position in the grave.

During the seventy-seven years, executions were carried out at Walton Jail, only two women were executed, the remaining sixty were men.

During the history of executions at Walton prison, it can be seen that over the years, there were five double executions at the prison, these were on the following dates;-

1. Tuesday, 2nd June, 1903.
2. Tuesday, 31st May, 1904.
3. Monday, 1st December, 1915.
4. Tuesday, 11th May, 1920.
5. Friday, 25th April, 1952.

In the present day, many of those condemned men and women who were executed at Walton Prison would have been released after a few years. Sentences in the present climate do not seem to reflect the fact that someone has had their life taken away, often in the most violent way.

Because of the advancement in Forensic Science, some

of these men and women executed, may even have been acquitted of the crimes for which they were sentenced to death.

Capital punishment was abolished by an Act of Parliament on 18th December, 1969. The last persons to be executed by hanging in the United Kingdom were Peter Anthony Allen and John Robson Walby (also known as Gwynne Owen Evans) for the murder of Alan West at Workington, Cumbria.

Allen was executed at Walton Prison, and Walby at Strangeways Prison, Manchester, on 13th August, 1964, at exactly the same time.

# EXECUTED AT WALTON PRISON

| | | |
|---|---|---|
| 1. | Elizabeth Berry | 14th March, 1887. |
| 2. | Patrick Gibbons | 17th August, 1892. |
| 3. | Cross Duckworth | 3rd January, 1893. |
| 4. | Margaret Walber | 2nd April, 1894. |
| 5. | John Langford | 22nd May, 1895. |
| 6. | William Miller | 4th June, 1895. |
| 7. | Elijah Winstanley | 17th December, 1895. |
| 8. | Thomas Lloyd | 18th August, 1897. |
| 9. | James Bergin | 27th December, 1900. |
| 10. | John Harrison | 24th December, 1901. |
| 11. | Thomas Marshland | 20th May, 1902. |
| 12. | Gustav Rau | 2nd June, 1903. |
| 13. | Willem Schmidt | 2nd June, 1903 . |
| 14. | Henry Starr | 29th December, 1903. |

15.  William Kirwin                31st May, 1904

16.  Pong Lung                     31st May, 1904

17.  Charles Patterson             7th August, 1907.

18.  See Lee                       30th March, 1909.

19.  Henry Thompson               22nd November, 1910.

20.  Thomas Seymour               9th May, 1911.

21.  Michael Fagan                 6th December, 1911.

22.  Joseph Fletcher              15th December, 1911.

23.  George Ball                  26th February, 1914.

24.  Joseph Spooner               14th May, 1914.

25.  John Thornley                 1st December, 1915.

26.  Young Hill                    1st December, 1915.

27.  William Hodgson              16th August, 1917.

28.  John Crossland               22nd July, 1919.

29.  William Waddington           11th May, 1920.

30. Herbert Salisbury      11th, May, 1920.

31. James Ellor      11th August, 1920.

32. George Wood      10th April, 1923.

33. James Winstanley      5th August, 1925.

34. Lock Ah Tam      23rd March, 1926.

35. James Leah      16th November, 1926.

36. William Robertson      6th December, 1927.

37. Albert Absolom      25th July, 1928.

38. Joseph Clark      12th March, 1929.

39. John Maguire      26th November, 1929.

40. Richard Hetherington      20th June, 1933.

41. Jan Mohamed      8th June, 1938.

42. Samuel Morgan      9th April, 1941.

43. David Williams      25th March, 1942.

44. Douglas Edmondson      24th June, 1942.

45. Ronald Roberts      10th February, 1943.

| | | |
|---|---|---|
| 46. | Thomas James | 29th December, 1943. |
| 47. | John Davies | 12th July, 1944. |
| 48. | Thomas Hendern | 17th July, 1946. |
| 49. | Walter Clayton | 17th August, 1946. |
| 50. | Arthur Rushton | 19th November, 1946. |
| 51. | Stanley Sheminant | 3rd January, 1947. |
| 52. | Peter Griffiths | 19th November, 1948. |
| 53. | George Semini | 27th January, 1949. |
| 54. | George Kelly | 28th March, 1950. |
| 55. | Alfred Burns | 25th April, 1952. |
| 56. | Edward Devlin | 25th April, 1952. |
| 57. | John Todd | 19th May, 1953. |
| 58. | Milton Taylor | 22nd June, 1954. |
| 59. | William salt | 29th March, 1955. |
| 60. | Richard Gowler | 21st June, 1955. |
| 61. | Norman Green | 27th July, 1955. |
| 62. | Peter Anthony Allen | 13th August, 1964. |

# THE BLACK CAP

In court the "Black Cap" would be placed on the Judge's head by the Clerk of the court and the final words pronounced.

> " The sentence of this court upon you is that you be taken from this place to a lawful prison, and thence to a place of execution, and there you suffer death by hanging, and that your body be buried within the precincts of that prison in which you will have been confined before your execution, and may the Lord have mercy on your soul."

# The Execution of Elizabeth Berry

On Monday, 6th, March, 1887, a party of twelve convicts were put to work in the Coach house at Walton Prison, Liverpool. The Coach house was a large wooden shed used for the storage of the prison vehicles.

Three sides of the building were covered, the remaining side was open to the elements, thus allowing anyone walking towards the building to see inside.

The convicts were to dig a "well" ten feet deep, ten feet wide, and twelve feet long. After the convicts had been returned to their cells, a team of bricklayers started to brick the side walls of the "well", after which the brick work was rendered with plaster.

A scaffold was then built over the "well" with a trap door which would allow the body of a condemned person to fall into the newly built room after execution.

The execution chamber was sixty yards from the condemned cell. Any inmate being sentenced to death would have to walk from the condemned cell and across the open yard into the execution chamber.

The gallows itself had been constructed on the level ground in which the convicted person would walk onto the trap door which would then be sprung by the executioner. The old way in which the condemned person would climb the steps to be executed was not used at Walton Prison.

The purpose of the gallows, was for the first execution that would take place at Walton Prison the following week. The prison had been open since 1855, but no executions had yet been carried out.

It would appear that the Prison Governor John Miles Anderson was expecting the condemned person to receive a reprieve from the death sentence. The reprieve was denied, and so the reason for the hastily erected execution chamber.

On Monday, 13th March, 1887, Elizabeth Berry, 31 years old stepped into the pages of Walton Prison history, when she became the first person to be executed at the prison for the murder of her daughter Edith Alice Berry, 11 years, at Oldham, Lancashire.

The last Sunday of Elizabeth Berry's life on earth was spent in the condemned cell with the prison Chaplain making her preparations for the following day.

The weather outside was very cold, snow was falling, and would freeze overnight making walking conditions the following morning very difficult.

The Chaplain left at 9 p.m. that evening, but returned at 6 a.m. the following morning. Mrs Berry was already awake, she had not slept much during the night, and was now talking to the female Prison Officers who had spent the night watching over her.

The story of how Elizabeth Berry came to be in this predicament was one which had left the whole country shocked.

Elizabeth Berry was employed as a nurse at Oldham Work House, Lancashire. Her husband had died five years previously leaving her to bring up two children from the marriage.

The children being a boy and a girl. The boy had died some fourteen months after his father.

Elizabeth at this point made arrangements for the

girl, Edith Berry, to stay with the sister of her deceased husband, Mrs Anne Sanderson, at her home in Miles Platting, Lancashire.

Mrs Berry was to pay her sister-in-law the sum of eight shilling a week to look after her daughter Edith. She also paid her one pence a week for insurance on the life of Edith.

In December, 1886, Mrs Berry applied for a Mutual Insurance for herself and her daughter for the sum of £100, which meant that in the event of one of them dying, the other received £100.

Since the death of her husband, Elizabeth had worked at a number of workhouses before being appointed to her present position.

The position of Nurse at Oldham workhouse also allowed the benefit of living on the premises in rent free accommodation.

The Medical Officer at the work house was Dr Patterson, who with Mrs Berry would hold the keys to the workhouse surgery.

On 27th December, 1886 Mrs Berry visited and stayed with her daughter Edith and sister-in-law Mrs Sanderson until 30th December, 1886.

When she returned to Oldham, her daughter Edith and a school friend of Edith's, Beatrice Hall, travelled with them.

The two children played happily in the building and grounds of the workhouse.

Edith Berry prior to travelling to Oldham was reported to be in fine health. A friendly child who was well liked by all who knew her.

| No. | Name | Date |
|---|---|---|
| 1 | Elizabeth Berry | 14 . 3 . 87 |
| 2 | Patrick Gibbons | 17 . 8 . 92 |
| 3 | Cross Duckworth | 3 . 1 . 93 |
| 4 | Margaret Walber | 2 . 4 . 94 |
| 5 | John Langford | 22 . 5 . 94 |
| 6 | William Miller | 4 . 6 . 95 |
| 7 | Elijah Winstanley | 17 . 12 . 95 |
| 8 | Thomas Lloyd | 18 . 8 . 97 |
| 9 | James Joseph Bergin | 27 . 12 . 1900 |
| 10 | John Harrison | 24 . 12 . 01 |
| 11 | Thomas Marsland | 20 . 5 . 02 |
| 12 | Gustav Rau | 2 . 6 . 03 |
| 13 | Willem Smith | 2 . 6 . 03 |
| 14 | Henry Bertram Starr | 29 . 12 . 03 |
| 15 | William Kirwan | 31 . 5 . 04 |
| 16 | Dong Lun | 31 . 5 . 04 |
| 17 | Charles Patterson | 7 . 8 . 07 |
| 18 | Lee Lee | 30 . 3 . 09 |
| 19 | Henry Thompson | 22 . 11 . 10 |
| 20 | Thomas Seymour | 9 . 5 . 11 |
| 21 | Michael Fagan | 6 . 12 . 11 |
| 22 | Joseph Fletcher | 15 . 12 . 11 |
| 23 | George Ball | 26 . 2 . 14 |
| 24 | Joseph Spooner | 14 . 5 . 14 |
| 25 | John James Thornley | 1 . 12 . 15 |
| 26 | Yang Hill | 1 . 12 . 15 |
| 27 | William Thomas Hodgson | 16 . 8 . 17 |
| 28 | John Crossland | 22 . 7 . 19 |
| 29 | William Waddington | 11 . 5 . 20 |
| 30 | Herbert Edward Rawson Salisbury | 11 . 5 . 20 |
| 31 | James Ellor | 11 . 8 . 20 |
| 32 | | |

Photo Stat copy of the Register of Death with the permission of the Governor of Walton Prison

FD 089768

**CERTIFIED COPY**
of an ENTRY
Pursuant to the Births and
Deaths Registration Act 1953

**Registration District** West Derby

1887. DEATHS in the Sub-District of Walton in the County of Lancaster

| No. | When and Where Died | Name and Surname | Sex | Age | Rank or Profession | Cause of Death | Signature, Description, and Residence of Informant | When Registered | Signature of Registrar |
|---|---|---|---|---|---|---|---|---|---|
| | (Col. 1) | (Col. 2) | (Col. 3) | (Col. 4) | (Col. 5) | (Col. 6) | (Col. 7) | (Col. 8) | (Col. 9) |

Certified to be a true copy of an entry in a register in my custody.

*Courtesy of Liverpool Record Office*

On Saturday, 1st January, 1887, Elizabeth was in another part of the building when Edith was violently sick. Elizabeth was seen a short time later trying to get Edith to drink a white milky fluid from a glass.

Dr Paterson who was in attendance at the workhouse examined Edith, he prescribed a mixture of iron and quinine.

Edith remained seriously ill throughout the remainder of the day. Dr Paterson continued to monitor Edith's condition.

The following day, Sunday, 2nd January, 1887 Edith appeared to be a little better. Dr Paterson informed Elizabeth that Edith was over the worse and should recover quickly.

At this point Dr Paterson noticed that a towel used by Edith had blood and vomit stains on it and on inspecting it further, he noticed that the towel had an acidic smell.

Dr Paterson borrowed Mrs Berry's key to the workhouse dispensary in order to prepare a bicarbonate mixture for Edith. At this time he saw that a bottle of creosote in the dispensary was empty.

He ordered Mrs Berry to obtain a new bottle and instructed her to give Edith a glass of water with a few drops of creosote mixed in the water.

Later that evening Edith's condition took a turn for the worse, she again started to be violently sick. Dr Paterson again attended, and saw that there were small blisters around the child's mouth.

Dr Paterson consulted with a second Doctor, both concluded that Edith had drunk a corrosive poison.

Edith's condition grew worse by the hour, she vomited up any medicine that she was given, she weakened rapidly.

On Monday, 3rd January, 1887, Mrs Sanderson received a telegram from Elizabeth Berry requesting that she travel to Oldham as her daughter Edith was dying.

Upon arriving at Oldham work house, Mrs Sanderson saw Edith was very ill, and was continually vomiting. Her mother Elizabeth was nursing her. It was hard to understand the change in her within a few days.

Throughout the night Edith got weaker by the minute, and at 5 a.m. the following morning she died.

Dr Paterson suspected that Elizabeth Berry had murdered her daughter by administering her two large doses of creosote. He refused to sign a death certificate, and a post mortem was carried out on the body of Edith.

Dr Paterson had asked Elizabeth, if she had any insurance on Edith, she had replied "not for a penny".

The post mortem results confirmed Dr Paterson's suspicions. The Police were informed and Elizabeth Berry was arrested and later charged with the murder of her daughter Edith Anne Berry.

Evidence quickly came to light that Elizabeth, did have her daughter insured for ten pounds, and had tried to get her insured for a further hundred pounds. The insurance company had rejected this last policy on behalf of Mrs Berry.

On 21st February, 1887, Elizabeth Berry appeared before Mr Justice Hawkins at Liverpool Assizes Court, the prosecution was conducted by Mr McConnell, and Mr Cottingham represented the defendant Berry who had pleaded not guilty to the crime.

The trial lasted four days, the main evidence was given by Dr Patterson, and the Doctor who had carried out the post mortem. The medical experts all agreed that the cause of death was a corrosive poison, namely the acid contents of the creosote.

The court was told about Mrs Berry having insured Edith, and then later denying the fact when questioned by Dr Paterson.

The jury having heard all the evidence in the case took just ten minutes to find Elizabeth Berry guilty of the wilful and malicious murder of her daughter.

The judge in passing sentence of death, remarked that a crime, so cold blooded, so merciless, and so cruel in causing the poor child to whom the prisoner had given birth to suffer so much pain and agony, passed all belief.

Mrs Berry was taken to Walton Prison to wait for the lawful sentence of the court to be carried out.

Mr Cottingham, the Barrister for the defence, travelled to London and submitted an appeal against the death sentence to the Home Secretary, who decided that in view of the horrific circumstances of the crime, the appeal could not be considered.

During the time Mrs Berry spent waiting for her sentence to be carried out, the authorities were having second thoughts on the cause of death of Mrs Berry's mother, with whom it had been proved she was living with at the time of her death.

The body of her mother, Mrs Mary Ann Finley was exhumed, and a post mortem revealed traces of an Atropine like substance in her body. A Coroners jury at Castleton returned a further verdict of murder against Elizabeth Berry.

In view of the sentence of death against Mrs Berry, it was

felt that a new trial for the murder of her mother would not be in the public interest.

She was not questioned over the deaths of her husband and son, although many people now suspected she had also murdered them.

On Sunday, evening 13th March, 1887, Mr James Berry (no relation) Public Executioner, arrived at Walton Prison. He was greeted by the Prison Governor John Miles Anderson, and shown to his quarters within the prison.

Mr Anderson informed him, that Elizabeth Berry had told the prison staff, that she was an old friend of the executioner, having met him at a Police Ball in Manchester some years before.

Later that evening James Berry went to the condemned cell, and upon looking through the cell inspection window, recognised Elizabeth from the Police Ball. He recalled having danced with her, and travelled home together for part of the journey.

On Monday, 14th March, 1887, large crowds of men and women gathered in Hornby Road, outside the gates of the prison, although the weather was freezing cold, with snow covering the ground.

At 7.45 a.m. as the prison clock started to chime, the Prison Governor, John Anderson, accompanied by James Berry, entered the condemned cell. Elizabeth Berry who was being attended by the Prison Chaplain, approached the executioner, and reminded him of their last meeting.

James Berry told her, that he did recall the evening, but it was some years ago and it was hard to recall it in much detail.

Mr Berry then pinioned her arms, and with the Prison

# Memorandum of Conditions to which any Person acting as Assistant Executioner is required to conform.

*(An Assistant Executioner will not be employed by the Governor without the concurrence of the High Sheriff.)*

1. An Assistant Executioner is engaged, with the concurrence of the High Sheriff, by the Governor of the prison at which the execution is to take place, and is required to conform with any instructions he may receive from or on behalf of the High Sheriff in connection with any execution for which he may be engaged.

2. A list of persons competent for the office of Assistant Executioner is in the possession of High Sheriffs and Governors : it is therefore unnecessary for any person to make application for employment in connection with an execution, and such application will be regarded as objectionable conduct and may lead to the removal of the applicant's name from the list.

3. Any person engaged as an Assistant Executioner will report himself at the prison at which an execution for which he has been engaged is to take place not later than 4 o'clock on the afternoon preceding the day of execution.

4. He is required to remain in the prison from the time of his arrival until the completion of the execution and until permission is given him to leave.

5. During the time he remains in the prison he will be provided with lodging and maintenance on an approved scale.

6. He should avoid attracting public attention in going to or from the prison ; he should clearly understand that his conduct and general behaviour must be respectable and discreet, not only at the place and time of execution, but before and subsequently ; in particular he must not give to any person particulars on the subject of his duty for publication.

7. His remuneration will be £1 11s. 6d. for the performance of the duty required of him, to which will be added £1 11s. 6d. if his conduct and behaviour have been satisfactory. The latter part of the fee will not be payable until a fortnight after the execution has taken place.

8. Record will be kept of his conduct and efficiency on each occasion of his being employed, and this record will be at the disposal of any Governor who may have to engage an assistant executioner.

9. The name of any person who does not give satisfaction, or whose conduct is in any way objectionable, so as to cast discredit on himself, either in connection with the duties or otherwise, will be removed from the list.

10. The apparatus approved for use at executions will be provided at the prison. No part of it may be removed from the prison, and no apparatus other than approved apparatus must be used in connection with any execution.

11. The Assistant Executioner will give such information, or make such record of the occurrences as the Governor of the prison may require.

*James Berry, he performed the first execution at Walton Prison on Elizabeth Berry (no relation) The date was 14th March 1887*

Governor leading the way followed by the Prison Chaplain reading the prayers for the dead.

The procession then proceeded from the condemned cell, Mrs Berry walked slowly behind the Chaplain, repeating the response to the prayers. Two female Prison Officers walked alongside the condemned woman. James Berry was next, followed by the three Prison Doctors.

The distance from the condemned cell to the execution chamber was sixty yards across an open yard. Sand had been sprinkled over the snow which had fallen on the ground.

Mrs Berry when nearing the execution shed, suddenly looked up from the ground, and upon seeing the gallows through the open end of the shed fainted. The Prison Officers assisted by James Berry caught hold of her. She was helped the rest of the way, and when placed on the scaffold again fainted.

At this point male Prison Officers took hold and supported her whilst executioner Berry completed his arrangements. She recovered consciousness whilst the cap was being pulled over her head, and called upon god to forgive her.

The trap door lever was pulled, and Elizabeth Berry dropped to her death.

A Coroner's Court was held at 10 a.m. the same day within the Prison, the jury returned a verdict that Elizabeth Berry had been duly executed in accordance with the sentence passed upon her by the court.

Elizabeth Berry was later buried within the Prison grounds.

Many people believed Elizabeth Berry was a serial killer, who had committed the crimes for the insurance money.

The authorities never questioned her about the other suspicious deaths in her family. She herself, never admitted being responsible for them. If she was, she took the secret to her grave.

## The Execution of Patrick Gibbons

From 7 a.m. on Wednesday, 17th August, 1892, a large crowd of people made their way up Hornby Road, Liverpool, and congregated outside Walton Prison.

The reason for this group of men and women being outside the prison was the execution of Patrick Gibbons, who had been convicted at the Assizes Court , St Georges Hall, Liverpool of the Murder of his mother Bridget Gibbons, on 9th July, 1892.

Police Inspector Hutchinson and a detachment of County Police Officers stood watch over the crowd. Nearby stood a Police vehicle ready to convey any dissenters away to the local station. The vehicle would not be needed this morning, the men and women stood around talking about the grim event that was about to take place the other side of the wall.

James Billington, the Executioner had arrived the previous evening, having travelled up from his home in Bury, Lancashire. He had been greeted by the Prison Governor, John Haverfield.

After viewing the gallows in the execution chamber, Billington settled into his accommodation, and after having a light meal, he visited the condemned man in his cell, and both men spoke of the following morning. Billington assured Gibbons the act would be swift.

After leaving the condemned cell, Billington returned to the execution chamber, and tested the trap door and scaffold from which the condemned man was to be hung. The scaffold had been erected at Walton Prison, after being removed from Kirkdale Prison which had recently closed.

Although many prisoners had been executed using the equipment at Kirkdale Prison, Billington made sure the gallows was in a state of readiness.

The condemned man Patrick Gibbons, 33 years, an ex soldier had spent the last few days talking and praying with the Prison Chaplain The Rev Father Birchall.

On Monday afternoon, he had met and talked, with his father and other members of his family. Tears flowed down the cheeks of Gibbons and his father, when the time came to say goodbye.

Gibbons had never denied that he had murdered his mother. He maintained he had been drunk, and could not remember the incident that was now, about to claim his life also.

At 7.45 a.m. on the morning of the execution, the prison bell began its monotonous toll. The sound signalled to the growing crowd outside the prison gates that the hour of execution was fast approaching.

At 7.50 a.m. the door of the prison opened and a Prison Officer beckoned to two reporters to follow him. These reporters were to witness the execution. The reporters were escorted to the coach house, in which the scaffold had been erected.

One wall of the coach house which had been converted into the execution chamber was open to the daylight. The floor of the chamber was partly wood, and partly brick. In the centre of the wooden floor boards, a white cross had been chalked onto the floor. High above the chalk mark was a wooden cross beam, with vertical supports. Dangling from the centre of the cross beam was a rope with a noose at the end.

A group of Prison Officers stood in a semi-circle facing the scaffold, nearby stood some prison officials, with the Under Sherriff of Lancashire, and Mr Elision, Justice of the Peace for Liverpool. The two reporters stood to the side. All present would have a good view of the forth-coming execution. Standing alone at this time was the Executioner, James Billington, leather straps hanging from his own leather belt.

In the condemned cell, Patrick Gibbons finished praying, and firmly shook hands with Father Birchall, and the two prison officers who had spent the last night of his life watching over him.

The Prison Governor John Haverfield entered the cell with the Prison Medical Officer, Dr Beamish, and seeing all was ready he gave his permission for the death procession to begin its grim march.

Father Birchall led the way, Patrick Gibbons two steps behind, a Prison Officer either side of him. Governor Haverfield and Dr Beamish walking at the rear of the party.

Just before 8 a.m. the silence in the execution chamber was broken by the sound of prayers for the dead, being said by Father Birchall who with the death procession approached and entered the room.

The members of the party then stood aside, and all eyes followed the movements of Executioner Billington. He positioned the condemned man on the chalk cross, removing the leather straps from his belt, he quickly and firmly pinioned Gibbons arms and legs with the straps and then covered the man's head with a white hood. He then placed the noose around Gibbons' neck and adjusted the knot.

Gibbons stood erect to attention, whist this was happening, trying to behave like an ex soldier. He was ready to meet his fate.

Billington glanced towards the assembled officials, and then suddenly pulled the trap door lever, the condemned man dropped from view.

The body of Patrick Gibbons like all before him, would remain hanging for an hour before being taken down. Dr Beamish would pronounce death had occurred.

The black flag was run up the prison flag pole, indicating to those outside, the execution had taken place.

The statutory notices were pinned up on the prison gates, stating that the  lawful execution of Patrick Gibbons had been carried out.

At 10 a.m. the Liverpool Coroner held the inquest into the death of Patrick Gibbons, the inquest jury were taken to view the body of the deceased man. The verdict of the jury was that death was strangulation due to hanging.

The body of Patrick Gibbons was buried within the grounds of the prison.

To find the reason for Patrick Gibbons' date with the hangman, we would have to travel back to 9th July, 1892, to the family home, at Water Street, Heyside, Royton, near Oldham. Gibbons lived at this address with his father and mother.

At 8 a.m. Gibbons father left his home to go to work, leaving his son at home with his mother, Bridget Gibbons, who even at this early hour was rather the worse for drink.

All seemed well when Mr Gibbons had left for work, all concerned were on good terms. At midday Mr Gibbons returned from work, but instead of going to his home, he called at the house of a neighbour, Mrs Russell, where he now found his son Patrick under the influence of drink.

After a short time Mr Gibbons returned to work, he for some reason never went to his own house. When he left, his son Patrick also left, and returned to his home.

Some hours later an argument was heard at the Gibbons house, between Patrick and his mother Bridget.

At 4 p.m. Patrick returned to the house of Mrs Russell, and said to her " Come and look at my mother, I have done it ". He then returned to his own house.

Mrs Russell along with another neighbour, Mrs Butterworth, went to the Gibbons' house, where they were met at the door by Patrick, who said to them " I have done it, I have cut her throat " .

The two women looked about, but could see nothing. Patrick Gibbons repeated his previous statement, and called on the women to follow him upstairs.

On going upstairs and into a bedroom, the two women saw the body of Bridget Gibbons lying on a bed with her throat cut.

A Doctor was summoned to the house, and after examining the body of Bridget Gibbons declared her dead. The Police were informed, and a short time later, Police Constable Thomas Ruston attended at the scene. Patrick Gibbons in the meantime just sat at the kitchen table, awaiting the arrival of the Police.

The Police Officer saw that there was blood on Gibbons' hands. Gibbon on seeing the Police Officer said " I am ready to go with you ". On the mantelpiece in the bedroom, a razor was found covered with blood.

After being arrested and taken to the local Police station for the crime, Gibbons said "I suppose I shall have to dance on nothing for this, I meant to do it, she was never sober. I shall soon be where I want to be, out of the road".

Gibbons was tried at the Liverpool Assizes Court on 29th July, 1892. He was represented by Mr Ford. The prosecution was conducted by Mr Yates and Mr Parry. The case was presided over by Mr Justice Denman.

The charge against Patrick Gibbons was having at Royton on 9th July, 1892, feloniously and of his malice aforethought killed and murdered Bridget Gibbons, his mother.

During the trial, his father gave evidence that his wife would normally drink a lot, and had once attempted to drown herself in a little pond, by lying on the floor, with her head in the water. She had also at one time, been committed to a lunatic asylum.

After hearing evidence, the jury retired for a short time, before returning with a guilty verdict.

Mr Justice Denman then passed sentence of death upon the convicted man.

In a space of five weeks, Patrick Gibbons had committed an offence of murder, he had been tried, convicted and executed. Swift justice even for these times.

# The Execution of Cross Duckworth

On 8th, November, 1892, the Lancashire village of Witton, near Blackburn was shocked at the violent death of a child.

Alice Barnes, aged 9 years, was the daughter of a Witton farmer. She attended the local school in the morning, but in the afternoon, she assisted her father about the farm.

On this particular afternoon, Alice had returned home from school, and after a light meal went to help her father on the farm. He asked her to drive some cows from one field on the farm to another.

During the short journey, she was seen by a number of her class mates who shouted and waved to her. Alice laughed, and waved back at her school friends.

She continued on her way, she drove the herd of cows across a small ford, but crossed the water herself by means of a small bridge.

A local man was seen standing on the bridge, by the school friends of Alice.

A short time later, a man was seen by a young boy carrying the body of Alice Barnes back across the bridge, which she had recently crossed.

Upon seeing the boy, the man dropped the girl's body and ran off. The young boy approached the girl's body, but was afraid to touch her, the boy also ran away.

At 1.30 p.m. the body of Alice Barnes was discovered by a neighbour of the dead girl. She saw that the child's clothing had been disturbed, and in her mouth was a handkerchief.

It was later discovered that Alice Barnes had in fact died from suffocation.

The Police attended at the scene, and immediately commenced a murder enquiry. A number of witnesses recalled a man running through the streets towards Blackburn, which was a short distance from the murder scene.

Within a short time, enquiries by the Police, led them to arrest and charge a local man Cross Duckworth with the murder of Alice Barnes.

Duckworth, 32 years, a Brass Dresser by trade, was a married man, with children. He resided with his family at Prince Street, Blackburn.

On 13th December, 1892, Cross Duckworth appeared at Liverpool Assizes Court. The trial was presided over by Mr Justice Grantham, and was to last two days.

Duckworth denied committing this dreadful crime. The evidence given by the defence was that Duckworth, at the time of the murder, was in the company of friends, some two hundred yards from the site of the murder.

After some deliberation, the jury found Duckworth guilty of the crime, but made a recommendation for mercy towards Duckworth on the grounds that the principal act, was not to murder young Alice Barnes, but to assault her.

The Judge waved aside this plea by the members of the jury, and passed sentence of death upon the convicted man.

Cross Duckworth was taken to Walton Prison to spend his last days, before being executed for this appalling crime.

On the Monday afternoon prior to his execution, Duckworth met with his wife and children in a room, near to the condemned cell. The meeting was an emotional one, with all concerned crying throughout.

The night leading up to the execution was one in which Duckworth had little sleep.

The Executioner, James Billington, had arrived the previous evening and had made his preparations for the forthcoming event.

On 3rd January, 1893, the weather was cold, some snow had fallen during the night, and remained on the ground.

Standing outside the red bricked walls of the prison, a small number of men and women had gathered near to the prison entrance, to await the grim proceedings that were about to take place a short distance away.

In the condemned cell, the Rev D Morris, the Prison Chaplain, was present with Duckworth; both men prayed together. Duckworth prepared himself for the ordeal ahead.

Duckworth although disappointed he had not received a reprieve was ready to meet his fate like a man.

At 7.45 a.m. the prison bell started tolling, the crowd outside the prison gates swelling in number by the minute stopped talking, knowing the time of death for Duckworth was fast approaching.

In the condemned cell, the Rev Morris took the leading position in the procession that formed. The condemned man, Cross Duckworth came next, a Prison Officer, either side of him. Executioner Billington was two steps behind him. The Prison Medical Officer Dr Beamish with the Prison Governor Mr Haverfield and the Chief Warder completed the formation.

The procession then proceeded the short distance to the execution shed, where the gallows stood waiting, the Rev Morris leading Duckworth in prayer.

Duckworth walked into the chamber and stood on the scaffold, looking about at the assembled officals. The High Sherriff of Lancashire at the head of this group had come to witness the lawful execution of this man, convicted of this awful crime.

Duckworth stood quietly, whilst Executioner Billington set about his work. Billington pinioned Duckworth's arms and legs with leather straps. A cloth hood was pulled over his face, the noose was adjusted around his neck.

Billington who had done this operation many times before, turned and looked towards the officals, and with a swift and smooth movement, pulled the trapdoor lever sending Cross Duckworth to his death.

The whole process from when Duckworth left the condemned cell to being hung took less than four minutes.

The black flag was run up the prison flag pole and would remain there until 9.00 a.m., signalling to those outside the prison that the sentence of the court had been carried out. Two notices were later pinned to the prison gate, one notifying that the execution had been carried out. This was signed by the High Sherriff of Lancashire. The second notice signed by the Prison Medical Officer confirmed the death of Duckworth.

The custom of letting the condemned persons body hang for one hour was allowed. After the body was taken down, it was taken to the hospital mortuary. The black flag was also lowered at this time.

At 10.30 hours the Coroner of Liverpool, Mr Sampson held the inquest into the death of Cross Duckworth. The jury were taken to the prison mortuary, and looked upon the body of the executed man.

All the officials present at the execution were called to give evidence. Dr Beamish gave evidence to the fact, that the cause of death was strangulation, and fracture of the neck.

The jury returned a verdict that Duckworth had been duly executed in accordance with the sentence passed down by the court.

*Walton Prison 1907*
*Courtesy of Liverpool Record Office*

# The Execution of Margaret Walber

On 16th November, 1893, Police Officers were summoned to attend at 6, Gildart Street, Liverpool, the home address of John Walber, and his wife Margaret.

John Murray, the son of Mrs Walber by a previous relationship, also resided in the premises.

The house was a large terrace style building, with the downstairs serving as a grocers shop, which was run by Mrs Walber. Upstairs a number of rooms were let out to several men, who lodged with the Walber family.

When the Police Officers were shown into a room, at the top of the house, by one of the men who lodged at the house, the sight that met the officers was a sickening one.

The body of John Walber was lying dead on the floor, the scene around him showing signs of a terrible struggle. The chamber pot was smashed, bits of glass were lying broken on the floor. The bed clothes were scattered all over the room. The walls, floor and clothing were covered with blood.

The lodgers were questioned as to what had occurred. One of the lodgers explained to the Officers that Mrs Walber had called to him, to come and see what had happened, and he and another man had gone upstairs and discovered the body of John Walber.

Mrs Walber who was present at the time had indicated, that her son John Murray was responsible for the crime. John Murray had left the house, his whereabouts were not known.

A post mortem examination took place on the body of John Walber, which discovered that his body was covered with awful gashes, which had bled considerably. The post mortem established he had died from shock and loss of blood.

Mrs Walber was taken to the Police station to make a statement and the Detectives discovered that her clothing was heavily bloodstained.

At the Police station, whilst being questioned about the death of her husband, Mrs Walber broke down, and admitted being responsible for his death. She made a full statement giving details of the events leading up to the death of John Walber.

It would seem that she had been married to John Walber for five years and she lived with him at the family home in Gildart Street, Liverpool.

The marriage was not a happy one, both were heavy drinkers, and continually argued and fought with each other, Margaret often coming out on top.

Some seventeen years earlier, John had been in a relationship with another woman, Ann Connolly who lived in Oakes Street, a short distance away. He had actually lived with her for some six weeks.

Since the relationship with Connolly had finished, John had not had any dealings with her until May, 1893. He had visited her, at her home, three or four times.

Margaret Walber had found out about her husband revisiting Ann Connolly, and had followed him, when he had next called on the lady. She had forced her way into the house and confronted both of them, threatening both with violence.

When John Walber had returned home, she had forced him upstairs to a top room in the house. She had removed all his clothes, and refused to let him leave the room, keeping the door fastened with a chain and padlock, she herself keeping hold of the key.

She often visited him in the room and other residents in the house would hear arguments taking place between the two of them. John Walber was heard to shout " I won't go there again ".

It would appear that Mrs Walber had kept her husband imprisoned for some four months and neighbours would often hear shouts of "murder" coming from the top room.

Lodgers living in the house saw John Walber twice in these four months. Mrs Walber explained to them that her husband had been visiting a house of ill-repute, and this was her way of dealing with the situation.

One neighbour who spoke to Mrs Walber, recalled her saying that her husband was upstairs, and the next time he came down, he would be carried down.

In the confession, Margaret Walber said, that on the day John died, her son had told her John had gotten hold of a pair of her son's trousers, and was now wearing them.

She had gone to the room, and removed the chain and padlock, she had then struck John on the head with the chain causing him to fall down.

John never moved after being struck down. She stated she was drunk at the time, and could not remember what else she had done. She did recall asking one of the lodgers to come and see her husband.

John Murray was traced to Dublin, and brought back to Liverpool. He explained that he had left the country, because he was so afraid of what he had seen on the day of the death of his stepfather John Walber.

*Top; Gildart Street early1900s*
*Bottom; Gildart Street today*

He was questioned for some time about these events. He stated that he had heard noises coming from the room his stepfather was in. He went upstairs to the room, and saw John Walber lying dead on the floor, his mother Margaret was standing looking down at John Walber.

John Murray had asked his mother who had done this and she had not replied. He had then left the room, and went down stairs, his mother Margaret following him down.

He had then left the house, travelling to Garston, before making his way to Dublin. Margaret Walber had given him four sovereigns prior to him leaving the house.

Police now charged Margaret Walber with the wilful and malicious murder of her husband.

On 20th November, 1893, Margaret Walber appeared at Liverpool Assizes Court and pleaded not guilt. She was remanded in custody for trial to Walton Prison.

On 5th December, 1893, Margaret Walber again appeared at Liverpool Assizes Court and was defended by Dr Cummins, M.P. who put forward a defence of Insanity due to the effects of alcohol on the day of John Walber's death. The defence was brushed aside by the court.

After a trial lasting six hours, she was found guilty of the wilful murder of her husband John Walber, she was sentenced to death.

The story of John Walber's imprisonment, and violent death so shocked the country, that no effort was made to obtain a reprieve for Mrs Walber who was resigned to her fate.

On Saturday, 31st March, 1894, the executioner James Billington arrived at Walton Prison. He remained in residence until Monday, 2nd April, 1894, when he would carry out the sentence of the court upon the convicted woman.

Mrs Walber was to spend her last few days being looked after by female officers. She would often be visited by the prison chaplain, the Rev Wade, who would lead her in prayer.

The subject of the murder was mentioned in the press nearly every day; domestic violence against the husband was most unusual even in these times.

At 8 a.m on Monday, 2nd April, 1894, Margaret Walber walked the short distance from the condemned cell to the execution room. She was escorted by Miss Gee (the Matron ) and several female officers.

During the time executioner Billington was pinioning her arms and legs, Mrs Walber was sobbing, the hood was placed over her head, the noose was put into position, and Margaret Walber was dispatched to her death.

The black flag was run up the prison flag pole, indicating to those outside the prison, that the sentence of the court had been carried out.

The usual certificates were pinned to the prison door, signed by the Prison Governor, and the Prison Medical Officer.

The inquest later held at the prison was informed by the executioner that the drop given to the woman was 6ft. 2 inches, death being almost instantaneous.

Dr Beamish, Prison Medical Officer stated death was due to fracture of the neck, and strangulation by hanging.

The execution according to the Prison Governor was performed in a successful and expeditious manner, there being no delay to the proceeding.

The body of Mrs Walber was kept in the prison mortuary, until burial by the Prison staff within the prison grounds.

## The Execution of John Langford

John Langford, 41 years, a Confectioner by trade, had separated from his wife, during the marriage; the couple had five children.

When the couple split up, the two eldest children remained with his wife, the three youngest children lived with their father, John Langford.

Mrs Langford appears to have moved from the area, no trace of her or the two children were ever found.

In July, 1892, John Langford met Elizabeth Stevens. She was an attractive young woman in her early20s. They both got on very well together, and after a short time, Elizabeth moved into the Langford home in Cockerell Street, Walton, Liverpool.

John had met Elizabeth at one of the local public houses that seemed to be on every street corner in those days. John liked to have a drink when he wasn't working night work in the local Bakery. Elizabeth it appears liked a drink, whatever the hour.

After Elizabeth moved in with John, all seemed well with the relationship; Elizabeth seemed to get on fine with the Langford children. The children in return, took to Elizabeth; they likened her to the mother they had lost. John Langford was happy that his domestic situation, had improved with the arrival of Elizabeth in his life.

After a few months the neighbours of the couple started to hear raised voicescoming from the house. On a number of occasions John Langford was heard to threaten Elizabeth.

It would appear that most of the arguments were about Elizabeth, who rather than watch over the children, had started going out drinking with her friends. It seemed Elizabeth had decided that domestic bliss was not for her. John Langford in the meantime continued working, providing for Elizabeth and his children.

The arguments between the two of them got steadily worse. Elizabeth would promise to stop going out drinking, but the minute John Langford left for work Elizabeth would be out drinking with her friends.

She would often arrive home completely intoxicated and end up being helped into the house.

On 2nd April, 1895, Elizabeth had been absent from the house most of the day and arrived home completely drunk, falling asleep on the floor in front of the fire.

John Langford by now had seen Elizabeth in this state on a number of occasions over the last three years. After seeing to his children he went off to work the night shift in the bakery, leaving Elizabeth where she was on the floor.

On returning home from the bakery the following day, he discovered Elizabeth was not at home. Upon going to look for her, he discovered her drinking in a public house on the corner of Florence Street. She was in company with two other women.

Langford angry confronted Elizabeth, and punched her in the face. She ran out of the public house pursued by Langford.

He caught up with her in a passageway at the rear of Cockerell Street, and stabbed her in the breast with a knife.

Elizabeth slumped to the ground, and at this point, Langford then attempted to cut his own throat.

People who had witnessed the incident called the Police,

who attended and had both Elizabeth Stevens and Langford removed to Stanley Hospital.

The Police questioned Elizabeth who stated that she had brought all the trouble upon herself by her own drunken conduct.

Sadly Elizabeth Stevens died later that day due to the injuries inflicted upon her by John Langford.

Langford was arrested and charged with the murder of Elizabeth. He admitted being responsible for the crime, and later appeared at the Assizes Court before Mr Justice Day. On the instructions of his Barrister, Mr Collingwood Hope, he entered a plea of not guilty.

The Prosecution case put to the jury was simple, after putting up for some time with Elizabeth's drunken spells, John Langford had had enough and finding her again missing from the house, he had tracked her down to a nearby public house, and after assaulting her in the full view of her friends he had chased after her, and stabbed her in the chest. She had later died from her injuries.

Mr Collingwood Hope defending Langford realised that his client would face the death penalty if convicted of this crime tried a different route with the jury.

He told the jury that Elizabeth Stevens' life was one in that in order to satisfy her craving for drink, she would constantly pawn things taken from the house. She was forever drunk, and neglecting her duties in the house. He pleaded with the jury that a verdict of manslaughter might be returned on the grounds that Langford was a passionate and caring man, who had committed this terrible crime in a "fit of rage" brought on by Elizabeth Stevens' actions.

The jury having listened to all the evidence returned a verdict of guilty of wilful murder.

Mr Justice Day in passing sentence remarked that it would have been impossible after listening to the evidence, for any man of common intelligence and honesty to have come to any other decision.

Langford was conveyed to Walton Prison to await for the lawful sentence of the court to be carried out.

A few days before his execution, Langford was allowed a visit with his three children in a room near to the condemned cell. The children had been staying with his sister since his arrest, but because she was ill, friends of Langford had brought them to see him. When the time came for the children to leave, tears flowed down Langford's cheeks, knowing he would never see them again, he pulled them close to him, and gave them each, one last hug.

On Tuesday, 22nd May, 1895, Langford after a good nights sleep, rose at 6 a.m. and attended mass in the prison chapel, given by the Rev David Morris. He prayed, asking for forgiveness for the dreadful crime he had committed.

Upon returning to the condemned cell, Langford continued talking in low whispers to the Rev Morris. The Prison Officers who had spent the last night with the convicted man, now joined him in prayers.

The Prison Governor Mr Walker had been waiting to see if a last minute reprieve came through from the Home Secretary now resigned himself to seeing the execution through.

At 7.30 a.m. the Governor was joined by the other officials who had come to witness the event. The executioner James Billington who had spent the night at the prison made one last inspection of the gallows, and trap door.

A large crowd had gathered outside the prison entrance, and because the murder was a domestic one, many people expected the death sentence to be overturned. They were to be disappointed; events the other side of the prison wall were moving to a  grim conclusion.

At 7.55 a.m. the Officials went to the condemned cell. After making sure all was in order, Langford's arms were strapped by executioner Billington. A procession lead by the Rev Morris then proceeded to the execution chamber.

Upon entering the room Langford walked onto the trap door, he continued following the Prison Chaplain in the prayers for the dead which delayed the execution by three minutes.

James Billington not wishing to rush the condemned man during his last minutes, stood nearby, waiting for the praying to end.

At 8.03 a.m. Billington strapped Langford's legs and feet, the white hood was pulled over his head, and with a swift pull on the trap door lever Langford was sent to his death.

The officials who witnessed the execution, noted that Langford appeared to die without pain. He had since his conviction acknowledged all along the justice of his sentence. He had expressed great regret for the crime he had committed.

At 11 a.m. the inquest into the death of the condemned man was held within the prison. The verdict was that John Langford had suffered death   through lawful execution.

Because Langford's sister was ill, and now unable to care for his children, they were placed in the care of Dr Barnardo's Homes. On the day prior to the execution, the children were sent to the London Homes, so as to escape from the final scene of their father's crime.

As with previous executions, Langford's body was buried within the grounds of the prison.

# The Execution of William Miller

People would normally pass the premises of 26, Redcross Street, Liverpool without giving a second glance.

The premises owned by Mr Edward Moyse , a bookseller, was also occupied by his young assistant John Needham.

The property was run down, business had not been too good the last few years, but Mr Moyse made enough though, to keep his head above water, always making sure that there was enough food in the house for John Needham and himself.

On the morning of 19th February, 1896, people passing up and down the street, were shocked when a young boy staggered out of the doorway of the address, and collapsed onto the pavement, blood dripping from a gaping wound on his head.

Men nearby rushed to help the young boy as he kept lapsing in and out of consciousness. The dockgate man who was first to reach the boy immediately recognised him as John Needham. He tried to question Needham as to what had happened to him.

He managed to tell the men that his master had been murdered by a man wearing blue clothes. This man who had been an acquaintance of Mr Moyse's, had also assaulted John Needham.

The Police by now had arrived at Redcross Street, and upon hearing the horrific tale, began a search of the premises.

The Officers soon discovered the body of the old bookseller. He had been butchered in his bed and it would appear a terrible fight had taken place in the room.

John Needham had by now been removed to the Northern Hospital and detectives waited at his bedside to question him.

For some days, Police Officers were unable to question John Needham, about what had happened at Redcross Street as his injuries although not life threatening were still quite serious.

When he finally did manage to speak to them he told them, he had been at home on the evening of 18th February, 1896, cooking a meal for himself. Mr Moyse was out for the evening but was expected to return home later on that night.

A man had called, and asked to speak to Edward Moyse, and was told Mr Moyse was not at home but would be home some time later. The man volunteered the information that he was a seafarer, and that he was an ex-lodger of Mr Moyse.

John Needham, not wishing to upset the man, agreed to let the stranger stay until Moyse returned home. The man also claimed that he wished to purchase some valuable books from Mr Moyse.

During the conversation, the man asked Needham, where his master kept his money, and did he have a bank. He mentioned that if the old man died suddenly, it would be awkward if nobody knew where he kept his worldly processions.

Needham told the man that he didn't know if Moyse had any money, as business had not been too good lately.

At 10 p.m. that evening Edward Moyse returned home and he immediately greeted the man. They both engaged in talk, sitting in the kitchen.

Needham at this point took his leave of the two men and retired to bed.

At 5 a.m. the following morning Needham was up, and preparing to dress himself, when the man entered the room, carrying a bucket and a hatchet. He asked the boy, where the coal was kept

Needham led the way to the scullery where the fuel was stored. The man at this time saw a trapdoor in the ceiling of the scullery and, standing on a chair, he climbed through the small opening, lighting his way with a candle which Needham had provided.

Needham laughing at the man's action, and hearing him crawling about in the loft, returned to his own bedroom.

Within a few minutes, the man came to Needham's room with the lighted candle. He blew out the candle, and at the same time, struck Needham a heavy blow to his head with the hatchet.

The young boy fell stunned onto the bed and the man now grabbed him around the neck, and attempted to choke him.

Needham was unable to recall what happened after that, but the next thing he knew, he was at the foot of the stairs, the strange man kicking him about the body. The man then threatened to kill Needham if he followed him.

Needham collapsed in the hallway and came round some time later, and upon entering the bedroom of Edward Moyse discovered the blooded and lifeless body of his employer.

He had somehow despite being seriously injured, managed to reach the street, and raise the alarm of the murderous attack.

Detective Chief Inspector Strettell, with the assistance of Detective Inspector Fisher took command of the Police squad that had been formed to trace the person responsible for this dreadful crime.

One vital clue John Needham was able to provide to the Police was that the assailant had a bad twitching movement on his face.

The description of the man with the twitching face, was given to the local newspapers who were more than happy to circulate it.

The people of Liverpool were spellbound by the violent murder, and were following the story, awaiting the publication of the day's newspaper with the latest instalment of the crime.

Soon information was given to the Police, which would lead them to arrest William Miller, who resided at 61, Edgeware Street, Liverpool.

Miller was interviewed by detectives who told the officers that on the night of the murder, he had been walking around the Garston and Gatearce areas of Liverpool, finally ending up in Kensington, a distance of some ten miles.

Blood stains were found on his clothing. He explained the stains away stating he had been working at the abattoir the previous Saturday.

The Police took Miller to the abattoir, and pointed out a room where he said he had been working . This albi was soon destroyed when the foreman at the abattoir was able to tell the Police that no animals had been killed at the abattoir on that day.

The Police next took Miller to the Northern Hospital, and put him on an identification parade before John Needham, who was still recovering from his injuries.

Needham at once pointed to Miller, identifying him as being the man with the twitching face who had attacked him in Redcross Street.

With this evidence, Miller was charged with the murder of Edward Moyse, and the attempted murder of John Needham.

Miller denied committing the offences, and appeared for trial before Mr Justice Hawkins at Liverpool Assizes Court on 13th May, 1895. After a trial lasting three days, Miller was found guilty and sentenced to death.

The Barrister representing Miller lodged an appeal against the capital sentence but this was later rejected by the Home Secretary.

Throughout his time in the condemned cell at Walton Prison, Miller continued to plead his innocence to the dreadful crime. He was visited by his wife and friends. He cried throughout the visit, all the tears being for himself, none for his victims.

On 4th June, 1895, the time of the execution was near. Miller had been told the previous day by the Prison Governor, Miles Walker, that his reprieve had been refused.

At 7.55 hours, William Miller was praying with the Rev Morris, when the Prison Governor, and James Billington, the executioner entered the condemned cell. Dr Beamish, the Prison Doctor, and his assistant had arrived some moments before.

William Miller stood quietly and allowed Billington to strap his arms, then following the Rev Morris, all the party proceeded to the execution room.

Billington guilded William Miller onto the white chalk

cross marked on the wooden planks of the trap door.

Within minutes Miller had been secured, the white cloth hood was pulled over his head and the noose was adjusted around his neck.

Billington being the professional that he was, wasted no time, the trap door lever was pulled and Miller was despatched to meet his maker.

The crowd on learning that the execution had taken place, started drifting away, but some stayed around the entrance to the prison hoping to see Billington leaving the prison, after his latest execution. He had become something of a celebrity.

Mrs Miller was well regarded by her neighbours, great sympathy was shown to her, from the time when her husband was arrested until his execution.

Some days after Miller's execution, the furniture, and household goods of Edward Moyse were sold by auction, for the sum of £23. It was a small price for a lifetime's work.

# The Execution of Elijah Winstanley

On Sunday, 29th September, 1895, two detectives from the Railway Police, lay in wait at Kays House railway sidings, about half a mile from Wigan railway station.

The Police Officers, Detective Sergeant Kidd of the Manchester Railway Police, and Detective Constable Osborne of the local Railway Police, were investigating thefts from railway wagons on the London and North Western Railway routes.

The enquiries made by the Officers led them to believe that the unmanned wagons were being raided whilst they were left in the Kays House sidings. The Officers had information that the offenders were local men.

At late evening the watching Police Officers saw a group of several men approach one of the stationary wagons and commence to cut open the tarpaulin which covered the property.

The Detectives rushed at the group of men, believing they would run off to avoid being arrested and the Officers hoped to detain one or two of them.

The several men although surprised by the Police Officers, did not run off but turned and attacked the Policemen, slashing at them with knifes. Both Officers drew their wooden staffs and attempted to defend themselves.

During the fight that ensued, Detective Sergeant Kidd was stabbed in the face and neck and fell to the ground dying. Detective Constable Osborne was seriously injured in the attack. The men ran off, and made good their escape

Detective Constable Osborne although badly injured, staggered to a signal box a short distance away, and raised the alarm.

Railway staff used a railway engine to return to the scene of the attack, where the body of Police Sergeant Kidd was discovered. Medical assistance was called for, and Dr Grahame attended at the scene, and pronounced Kidd to be dead.

Constable Osborne by now had collapsed, due to his injuries, and was taken to Wigan Infirmary.

The body of the dead Police Officer was taken aboard the railway engine, and removed to Wigan Railway Station.

The Police were now informed, and Superintendent Brassington of the Wigan County Police Division attended with a detachment of Officers.

A search of the murder scene found the weapons that had been used to inflict the injuries to the deceased Officer, and four hats and a scarf were also recovered.

News of the murderous attack upon the Police Officers soon spread throughout the area.

Nearly fifty Police Officers worked throughout the night to arrest the persons responsible for this dreadful crime.

Within hours five men had been arrested in connection with the crime, amongst them William Kearsley, well known to the local Police and Richard Pritchard. The men were taken to Wigan Infirmary, and placed before Detective Osborne who immediately identified Kearsley as being one of his attackers.

Later that day, the five men appeared before Wigan Police Court and were remanded in custody. When asked if they had any objection to being remanded, Kearsley stated that he knew nothing of the affair.

Police enquiries continued through out the following day, information led the Police to a man named William

Halliwell of Kays Houses. His home was watched throughout the day in the hope of apprehending him.

Halliwell was later seen in company with a group of men in a field close to his home. Police Officers moved in, with the intention of detaining him. It would appear that Halliwell knew the Police were after him and he ran off and made his way to his home.

He was arrested at his home within minutes by Police Inspector Longworth, and Sergeant Wilcock of the County Police. He was handed over to the Borough Police, who under Superintendent Macintosh, had taken responsibility for investigating the crime.

Halliwell was at once taken to Wigan Infirmary, and put on a identification parade with six other men in the line up.

The injured Officer, Detective Osborne, was brought in to view the parade and he immediately picked out Halliwell as being one of the men who had attacked him.

Detective Osborne pointed out Halliwell, stating " That is the man who took my staff ". He then said if you pull up his trousers, you will see bruising on his leg.

Superintendent Macintosh ordered Halliwell to pull up his trouser legs and on his left leg heavy bruising could be seen, the marks similar to a Police wooden staff.

Halliwell was later charged with being implicated with the attack upon the two Officers and he appeared before Wigan Police Court and was remanded in custody.

Halliwell by now realising the seriousness of his position decided to make a statement outlining his part in the attack upon the officers.

It would appear that Halliwell, and three other men Richard Pritchard, William Kearsley and Elijah Winstanley had been drinking in a public house known as the New Inn. After having a few drinks, the four men, all employed as Colliers, decided to proceed to a second public house, known as The Fox.

On route to The Fox public house, the men crossed the Kays House railway sidings, the property of Lancashire and Yorkshire Railways Company. The men decided to see what they could steal from the railway wagons that were parked nearby.

Richard Pritchard at this time had second thoughts and left the other three men who proceeded to where the wagons were parked.

At the wagons Halliwell kept watch whilst Kearsley and Winstanley set cutting the tarpaulin that covered the goods in the railway wagon. The two Police Officers had now come upon the three men and a fight took place.

Halliwell fought with Detective Osborne and whilst he was fighting him Kearsley had come up and kicked Detective Osborne. Whilst he was on the ground Kearsley had run off and then Halliwell took the opportunity to break free and also ran off.

He stated that whilst he was fighting Osborne, the other two men, Winstanley and Kearsley, had been fighting with Detective Sergeant Kidd. He stated he had no idea what had occurred in this other fight.

This statement corresponded with one, later made by Detective Constable Osborne, but he added that Winstanley had also come up to him and had been struck by Osborne using his Police wooden staff.

The Police now had the full story of the events leading up to the attack upon the two Officers in the railway sidings.

Within hours Police had arrested Elijah Winstanley and he admitted committing the crime, saying he had stabbed Detective Sergeant Kidd. He was later charged with the offence, and appeared before the Police Court with all the other arrested men.

Elijah Winstanley, William Kearsley and William Halliwell were remanded in custody. The other men were released, the Police offering no evidence against them.

Detective Constable Osborne was able to say in his statement, that after the men had run off, although seriously injured himself, he had gone in search of his fellow Police Officer, and had discovered him a short distance away.

Detective Sergeant Kidd still alive at this time, had enquired "Is that you Osborne? Get me a drink of water".

Although badly injured himself, Detective Osborne attempted to carry Kidd out of the railway yard. He was unable to do this, and leaving Detective Sergeant Kidd, he staggered to the signal box and raised the alarm.

The funeral of Detective Sergeant Kidd was held at Salford Cemetery on 3rd October, 1895. The funeral procession walked behind the coffin from the deceased man's home in Zebra Street to the cemetery. Mrs Ellen Kidd carried the youngest of her seven children, a child of some twelve weeks.

Some ten thousand people turned out in Salford to watch the Police Officer's last journey. The sight of his children stood around his grave moved many of them to tears.

On 26th October, 1895, the accused men appeared at Liverpool Assizes Court charged with the murder of Detective Sergeant Robert Kidd. William Halliwell had now turned "Queens evidence" and would speak against Winstanley and Kearsley.

Both were found guilty and were sentenced to death. Winstanley before leaving the dock stated that he alone had inflicted the injuries to the deceased. He stated that Kearsley had no part in this murderous deed.

This was to put a complexion on the matter because, Halliwell had told of Winstanley speaking to him later that evening in the Fox public house, and saying that he, Winstanley, had stabbed Kidd whilst Kearsley had held him.

Both men were conveyed to Walton Prison to await for the sentence of the court to be carried out.

Both men appealed against the death sentence.

The Governor of Walton Prison, Mr Miles Walker, later received correspondence from the Home Office, stating that on the advice of the Home Secretary, her Majesty had been pleased to commute the sentence of death passed upon William Kearsley at Liverpool Assizes Court to penal servitude for life.

Further correspondence was received stating that after full consideration of the case of the man Elijah Winstanley, who was condemned to be hanged on the 26th October, 1895, for the murder of Railway Detective Robert Kidd at Wigan on the 29th September, 1895, the Home Secretary has expressed regret that he cannot see his way to advise her Majesty to grant a reprieve.

Mr James Wilson, the Solicitor who had acted on behalf of Winstanley received a similar letter.

On being informed of the decision made by the Home Secretary, Winstanley was said to have completely broken down. He walks non-stop around his cell, and is unable to eat or sleep.

He attends church twice a day, and spends a lot of time with the Prison Chaplain.

The Prison staff in the meantime carried on making the preparations for the execution. James Billington was expected to be the executioner, and a room had been prepared for him.

On Tuesday, 17th December, 1895, a crowd of some three hundred people had gathered in Hornby Road, outside the prison.

Some members of the assembled crowd had travelled from Wigan. Whether they were friends of Winstanley it is not known.

At 7.55 a.m. the condemned man was escorted to the execution room by Prison Officials. He had been pinioned by executioner Billington and despatched to meet his maker at 7 a.m. The execution had proceeded without incident. The condemned man although quiet, had resigned himself to his fate.

Once the black flag was run up the prison flag pole, signalling that the execution had taken place, the crowd quickly dispersed from Hornby Road.

An inquest was held at the Prison later that day, the jury returning a verdict in accordance with the evidence, that death was due to hanging, and that the law had been duly executed and carried into effect.

William Halliwell was released by the court as a result of him turning Queens evidence. He returned to live in Wigan. What became of him is not known.

# The Execution of Thomas Lloyd

Thomas Lloyd and his wife, Julie Ann Lloyd were well known to the Police. Officers had been called to 39, Tillard Street, Liverpool, the Lloyd family home on a number of occassions.

Both Thomas and his wife Julie were heavy drinkers, and would often be violent to each other. Their married life was not a happy one, visits to the local public houses being the only escape from their dreary life.

Thomas Lloyd and his wife occupied rooms on the first floor at Tillard Street, a family named McDowell also rented rooms on the same floor.

In fact Mr and Mrs McDowell had on many occasions become involved in the violent arguments between Thomas and his wife.

A number of times both the McDowells had received blows from the fighting couple whilst trying to keep them apart.

On the evening of 19th June, 1897, Thomas Lloyd, 55 years, a Boilermaker by trade, returned to the family home. He had been absent for a week.

He had called in at his local public house before arriving home, and drank five or six pints of beer. He confided to some friends, Mr and Mrs Gray who lived in nearby Chelmsford Street, that he was afraid to go home, as his wife would not let him in.

Mrs Gray knowing of the history between Lloyd and his wife, agreed to walk to his home with him, and attempt to mediate with Mrs Lloyd.

Upon reaching 39, Tillard Street, Thomas entered the

house and was instantly attacked by Julie Lloyd, who also appeared extremely drunk.

Julie Lloyd claimed that Thomas Lloyd's absence for a week was proof of his unfaithfulness. Mrs Gray having seen the couple argue, left the house almost immediately

The arguing between the two lasted for some considerable hours, before Julie Lloyd decided she had had enough and was off to bed.

Mrs McDowell who shared the house with the Lloyd family was in bed across the landing. She was awake and listening to every word that was said by Thomas and Julie.

Julie Lloyd was heard to say "I'm off to my bed". She then called Thomas an offensive name. Thomas Lloyd at this time shouted, "I will finish you and the other ----- too." He then left the room and went downstairs.

Mrs McDowell could hear Thomas searching about in the kitchen area. After a few minutes he returned back upstairs and on the way to his own room, he opened the door of the McDowell's room and looked in.

Mrs McDowell saw that Thomas had a hatchet in his hand. He never spoke and turned away, perhaps thinking Mrs McDowell was asleep, and went to his own room, where his wife was in bed.

Mrs McDowell looked across into the Lloyd's bedroom, and saw Thomas Lloyd standing over his wife. He then struck out four or five times with the hatchet. He shouted at his wife "I'll cut the head off you". He then left the room, and went downstairs and slept in the kitchen.

In the meantime Mrs McDowell frightened for herself and her child, locked her bedroom door and did not leave the room until the next morning.

At 8 a.m. the following morning she looked into the Lloyd's bedroom and saw Julie Lloyd lying on the bed, her head was a dreadful sight. She had deep wounds on her head and blood stains covered the bed clothes. The wounds appeared to have been inflicted with the hatchet.

The Police were called, and Julie Lloyd was removed to the local hospital. A search of the house and surrounding area failed to locate Thomas Lloyd.

Thomas Lloyd was finally arrested by Police on 24th June, 1897. On his way to the Police station, Lloyd said to the arresting Officer "I did it, if I have to be hung, I'll swing like a man".

When he was later charged, Lloyd said "No never, I never struck her, no-one ever saw me strike her".

Julie Lloyd remained in a serious condition in hospital. She never regained consciousness and on 26th June, 1897, she died from her injuries.

Thomas Lloyd was now charged with the wilful and malicious murder of his wife.

Friends of Lloyd rallied round and raised the sum of 30 shillings to provide a Solicitor to help the accused man. Unfortunately the person charged with holding the money, failed to employ a Solicitor to act on behalf of Lloyd. What became of the money is not known.

On 30th, July, 1897, Thomas Lloyd appeared before Liverpool Assizes Court, in St George's Hall, charged with the murder of Julie Lloyd on 19th June, 1897.

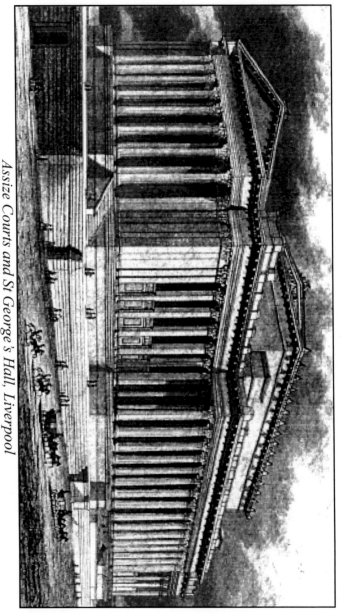

*Assize Courts and St George's Hall, Liverpool*
*Courtesy of Liverpool Record Office*

Mr Justice Bruce presided over the court, the prosecution was conducted by Dr O'Feely and Mr Gibson. At the request of the Judge Mr Dowdall represented the defendant Lloyd who had pleaded not guilty to the offence.

At the conclusion of the trial Mr Dowdall addressed the jury on behalf of Lloyd, he submitted that the death of the woman was as a result of a drunken quarrel, and subject to the direction of his Lordship, they might infer there was no deliberate attempt to murder Julie Lloyd.

The jury after deliberating for some twenty minutes returned a verdict of guilty of wilful murder.

His Lordship in passing sentence of death upon Lloyd, said the prisoner had been convicted upon the clear evidence of a most cruel and savage attack upon his wife.

Lloyd displayed no emotion on hearing the sentence and walked quietly from the dock to the cell below.

Thomas Lloyd was to spend the last few weeks of his life in the cell kept for condemned inmates at Walton Prison, Liverpool.

Whilst in prison waiting for the sentence of the law to take its course, Lloyd's case was taken up by Mr W.H.Quilliam, a Solicitor from Manchester Street, Liverpool.

Mr Quilliam set about preparing a petition for the commutation of the capital sentence that had been passed upon Thomas Lloyd. He had a number of witnesses interviewed who provided history of the violent and drunken relationship of Thomas and Julie Lloyd.

A number of tables were set up in various locations in Liverpool to enable people to sign the petition. Over 9,000 people stopped at these tables and signed the petition to save the condemned man.

This large petition together with the statements were sent to the Home Secretary in the hope of a reprieve for Thomas Lloyd.

Friends who visited Lloyd in prison kept him informed of the crusade to have the death sentence commuted. The prisoner seemed upbeat at the efforts to save him.

On 17th August, 1897, Mr Quilliam received a letter from the Secretary of State, saying that after duly considering the circumstances of the case of Thomas Lloyd, and the memorials and statements forwarded by you on his behalf, regrets that he can see no sufficient grounds for advising any interference with the due course of the law. The execution will therefore take place tomorrow morning.

At 8 a.m. on Wednesday, 18th August, 1897 Thomas Lloyd was executed. He had risen at 6 a.m. and ate a light breakfast. He caused executioner James Billington no problems, walking to the gallows without any assistance.

The several hundred people who had braved the wet weather watched the black flag being raised up the prison flag pole. Some stayed behind to read the death notice that was pinned to the prison gate.

The detachment of Police Officers who had been deployed outside the prison in Hornby Road were able to return to the Police station - no incidents had taken place.

The inquest held at the prison gave a verdict that the death was due to dislocation of the vertebrae, caused by hanging, death was instantaneous.

The sentence had been carried out in accordance with the law.

# The Execution of James Bergin

James Joseph Bergin, 28 years, a grocers assistant, living in Crete Street, off Great Homer Street, Liverpool, had been courting his girlfriend Margaret Morrison for some three years.

Margaret, 24 years old, was a pretty girl who resided with her parents in Brazenose Road, Bootle.

The relationship had gone well at first, Bergin was always welcome at the Morrison home. The couple had become engaged, and set a date for their wedding.

Within weeks of setting the wedding date the relationship started to turn sour. The arguments were mostly over religion - Margaret was a protestant, and Bergin, Irish born was a catholic. Bergin's family objected to him marrying a protestant

The arguments became more serious, Bergin started making threats to kill Margaret. In March, 1900, the engagement was broken off, and Bergin was refused entry to the Morrison home.

The family had become concerned about the threats Bergin was making to Margaret.

On 25th March, 1900 Bergin had called at the Morrison home, and after being told by Mrs Morrison her daughter was not at home, Bergin had told her, if he could see Margaret just for one more time he would not bother her again. Mrs Morrison relented and let Bergin into the house.

Shortly after Bergin left, a revolver was found in the grid opposite the house.

Mrs Morrison questioned Margaret about the weapon

and she admitted she had put it in the grid, after taking it from Bergin.

She went on to tell her mother that the previous evening she was with Bergin and he had asked her to marry him, but when she had refused, he had pointed the revolver at her, and pulled the trigger, but he had missed her. She had escaped by running into a house. He had only called to see her, to check if she had been injured.

Bergin although upset about the break-up of his relationship with Margaret, decided the best course of action was to put his broken engagement behind him, and return to his family in Rathdrum, County Wicklow.

Within weeks, James Bergin returned to Liverpool, and tried to rekindle his romance with Margaret and after a few weeks the relationship was back on.

The Morrison family were fed up with Bergin's mood swings, and the situation as Bergin was still threatening Margaret.

Margaret's parents persuaded her to finish with Bergin as they were very concerned for her safety

Towards the end of July, Bergin called at the Morrison home in Brazenose Road, Bootle. Although Margaret was not at home, Bergin was allowed to wait in the parlour for her. When she returned home, Bergin and Margaret stayed in the parlour talking.

Mrs Morrison heard the sound of a struggle, and on going to see what had occurred, saw bits of a broken bottle on the floor, Bergin's trouser leg was ripped, and what appeared to be a burn was on his leg. Margaret told her that the bottle had contained carbolic acid.

Mrs Morrison sent for the older brother of Bergin, who

on arrival at the Morrison home, had a heart to heart talk with his brother, before taking him home.

Between July, and October, Bergin continued to meet with Margaret, the relationship was in a sort of on-off mode.

On 20th October, 1900, Bergin called at Brazenose Road. He was drunk and was told by Mrs Morrison that Margaret was not at home.

Bergin said to her,"She is your daughter, but remember, she will never walk out with any other man." He left the house a short time later.

The following Saturday, 27th October, 1900, Margaret and her mother, went shopping to Ranelagh Street, Liverpool During the day they met up with Bergin and a short time later they were joined by Mr Morrison.

At 8.30 p.m. Margaret's mother and father left them to walk home to their house in Bootle. Margaret and James Bergin were to remain out, to go to a place of entertainment.

At 11 p.m. that evening, a number of witnesses saw Margaret and Bergin in Bankhall Street, walking towards the Morrison home. They both seemed to be getting along fine.

One witness, Margaret Cochoran, spoke to them, saying they were arm in arm. She knew Margaret Morrison and had wished them both goodnight.

A short distance away, she had heard the sound of a Police whistle, coming from the direction she had just walked. She went back and saw the body of a woman lying on the ground.

Cochoran at this point ran to the Morrison home to see if Margaret Morrison was at home. On discovering she wasn't, this confirmed her suspicion, that the injured woman was Margaret. By the time she returned to the scene a large crowd had gathered.

A number of witnesses saw the couple walking in Bankhall Street, they had seen the flash from the gun being fired, and they had then seen the man bend down and fire a second time at the head of the woman.

The man had then run off, one of the witnesses had chased him, and attempted to trip him up. The gunman managed to evade him, and escape from the scene.

Word had now reached the Morrison family who attended at the scene, and saw the unconscious body of their daughter, being supported by Police Officers who were kneeling beside her.

Margaret Morrison was moved to Stanley Hospital, where doctors discovered she had two bullet wounds to her head.

The gun that caused the wounds had been placed so close to her head, it had caused burn marks to her skin. She was in a very serious condition, the doctors treating her, didn't think she would live.

A team of Detectives led by Detective Inspector Lamothe commenced enquiries, to trace and arrest James Bergin.

At 4.45 p.m. on Sunday, 28th October, 1900, as a result of enquiries, Police Officers attended at 24 Howe Street, Bootle, the address of a Mrs Coleman, a relative of James Bergin.

At this address which was occupied by some twenty men, Detective Sergeant Lindsay arrested James Bergin. He was brought from the premises with some difficulty, because the large group of men attempted to assist him in spite of the serious nature of the crime.

Bergin was later interviewed and charged with the attempted murder of Margaret Morrison. He replied " I have nothing to say ".

Later that evening Detective Sergeant Aspin went to 20, Crete Street, Liverpool, the home address of Bergin. In a coat pocket in Bergin's bedroom, five bullets were recovered.

Bergin had resided at the address for some three years, his brother who owned the house was a serving Police Officer.

On Monday, 29th October, 1900, Bergin appeared before John Kingborn, Deputy Stipendiary Magistrate, at the Police Court, Dale Street, Liverpool and he was remanded in custody.

Later that evening Margaret Morrison died from her injuries, her parents were with her to the end.

On Tuesday, 30th October, 1900, Bergin again appeared before court, when the charge against him was amended from one of feloniously wounding to one of wilful murder. He was again remanded in custody.

Bergin later appeared before Mr Justice Darling at Liverpool Assizes Court. The Prosecution was conducted by Mr Sanderson and Mr Leslie Scott. Bergin was defended by Mr Rigby Swift.

Bergin pleaded not guilty to the offence. Mr Swift put forward the defence, that Bergin was not responsible for his actions at the time he took Margaret Morrison's life.

After deliberating for an hour, the jury returned a guilty verdict, but made a strong recommendation of mercy.

Mr Justice Darling before inferring upon Bergin, the final penalty of the law, that enacts a life for a life, said the jury had rejected the idea that the man he was addressing was insane. Every action he did, said Mr Justice Darling was evidence of his perfect sanity, and his extreme malice against the woman, whose life had been forfeited. Because his relations were not of her religion, and objected to his marrying her, and after the engagement was broken off, he persecuted her with his affections.

When he could not marry her, he determined that no-one else should. Having come to that decision, he armed himself with a fatal weapon, and murdered her by firing two bullets into her head.

Bergin was taken to Walton Prison to await the lawful sentence of the court.

Whilst in prison, Bergin's Barrister petitioned the Home Secretary for a reprieve on behalf of his client. This was refused; Bergin would pay the full penalty.

On Wednesday, 27th December, 1900, a cold brisk wind was blowing across the prison. A large crowd of some eight hundred people braved the cold morning to stand outside the prison.

At 8 a.m. Joseph Bergin was executed by James Billington, the execution was swift, Bergin had been a model prisoner since being sent to Walton Prison, the staff who had looked over him expressed a great sympathy towards him.

He had met his death in a manly way, he showed no sign of remorse towards the victim, or her distraught family.

*Bankhall Street, junction with Brazenose Road.*
*Location of the murder of Margaret Morrison.*
*Pictured in background; Brazenose Road cafe, formerly*
*The Hangman's Public House*

# DIETARIES

(1884)

## CLASS 1.

Prisoners confined for any Term not exceeding Three Days.

| MALES. | | FEMALES. |
|---|---|---|
| Breakfast | . 1 pint of Oatmeal Gruel. | 1 pint of Oatmeal Gruel. |
| Dinner | . 1 lb. of Bread. | 1 lb. of Bread. |
| Supper | . 1 pint of Oatmeal Gruel. | 1 pint of Oatmeal Gruel. |

## CLASS 2.

Convicted Prisoners for any term exceeding Three Days, and not exceeding Fourteen Days.

| MALES. | | FEMALES. |
|---|---|---|
| Breakfast | 1 pint of Oatmeal Gruel & 6 oz. of Bread. | 1 pint of Oatmeal Gruel & 6 oz. of Bread. |
| Dinner | 12 oz. of Bread. | 6 oz. of Bread. |
| Supper | 1 pint of Oatmeal Gruel & 6 oz. of Bread. | 1 pint of Oatmeal Gruel & 6 oz. of Bread. |

Prisoners of this Class employed at hard labour to have, in addition, one pint of Soup per week.

## CLASS 5.

Prisoners employed at hard labour for terms exceeding Three Months.

### SUNDAY, TUESDAY, THURSDAY AND SATURDAY.

| MALES. | | FEMALES. |
|---|---|---|
| Breakfast | 1 pint of Oatmeal Gruel & 6 oz. of Bread. | 1 pint of Oatmeal Gruel & 6 oz. of Bread. |
| Dinner | 4 oz. } Cooked Meat, without bone. | 3 oz. of { Cooked Meat, without bone. |
| | 1 lb. of Potatoes and 5 oz. of Bread. | ½ lb. of Potatoes and 6 oz. of Bread. |

# DIETARIES.

(1884)

## MONDAY, WEDNESDAY AND FRIDAY.

| | | |
|---|---|---|
| *Breakfast* | 1 pint of Cocoa, (Made of ½ oz. of flaked Cocoa or Cocoa Nibs, sweetened with ¾ oz. of Molasses or Sugar) & 6 oz. of Bread. | 1 pint of Cocoa (Made of ½ oz. of flaked Cocoa or Cocoa Nibs, sweetened with ¾ oz. of Molasses or Sugar) & 6 oz. of Bread. |
| *Dinner* | 1 pint of Soup. 1 lb. of Potatoes. 6 oz. of Bread. | 1 pint of Soup. ½ lb. of Potatoes. 6 oz. of Bread. |

Supper the Seven Days,—1 pint of Oatmeal Gruel, and 6 oz. of Bread.

### CLASS 6.

*Convicted Prisoners not employed at hard labour for periods exceeding Fourteen Days, same as Class 4.*

### CLASS 7.

*Prisoners sentenced by Court to solitary confinement, same as Class 6.*

### CLASS 8.

*Prisoners for examination, before trial, and misdemeanants of the first division, who do not maintain themselves, same as Class 4.*

### CLASS 9.

*Destitute Debtors, same as Class 4.*

### CLASS 10.

*Prisoners under punishment for prison offences for terms not exceeding Three Days, 1 lb. of Bread per diem.*

*Prisoners in close confinement for prison offences under the provisions of the 42nd section of the Gaol Act.*

| | MALES. | FEMALES. |
|---|---|---|
| *Breakfast* | 1 pint of Oatmeal Gruel & 8 oz. of Bread. | 1 pint of Oatmeal Gruel & 6 oz. of Bread. |
| *Dinner* | 8 oz. of Bread. | 6 oz. of Bread. |
| *Supper* | 1 pint of Oatmeal Gruel & 8 oz. of Bread. | 1 pint of Oatmeal Gruel & 6 oz. of Bread. |

## The Execution of John Harrison

On Christmas Eve, 24th December, 1901, people all over Liverpool were waking up to a cold rain-filled winters day.

In Walton Prison, some four miles from Liverpool city centre, this was not just an ordinary day, the whole prison was on standby for the execution that morning of John Harrison.

The condemned man, a collier by trade, was a native of Parr, St Helens.

In February, 1901, he married a woman named Alice Ann Wright. He had known Alice for some three months before he decided to settle down and make his future with her. Alice, though had not been entirely honest with John, failing to mention that she was still married to James Wright, a fishmonger from Fleetwood.

She was separated from James Wright because of her own misconduct. She had in fact been caught playing around with other men, and so hence the reason for her failed marriage.

The relationship between the couple got off to a bright start, both parties seemed very happy together.

On 26th July, 1901, both John and Alice called upon Mr Marsh, a farmer from Rose Farm, Bickerstaff, Lancashire, with a view to renting a cottage on Rose Farm.

The parties agreed to the rental, and at 10 a.m. on 27th July, 1901, Mr Marsh met the couple at the cottage and, after showing them around the property, left them with the keys.

*Female members of staff at Walton Prison. I have been unable to identify them. What I do know is that the top photo is dated approx 1900/1901. The other two are about the 1920s.*

Both John and Alice appeared to be on good terms when Farmer Marsh had left them.

At 12. 30 p.m. that day, John Harrison was met by another collier, who reported that John seemed to be hurrying away from the cottage.

Some thirty minutes later, a young girl passing the cottage saw that the windows had been broken and, on investigating further, she discovered the body of Alice Wright lying on the floor of the cottage.

The Police were informed and commenced a search to trace John Harrison who had not been seen since 12.30 p.m. that day.

At 9 p.m. that evening, John Harrison called on Mr Marsh. He told the farmer that he had been to Skelmersdale and on returning home he had found his wife dead.

Harrison had met with a number of people during the day and had told them he had been with Alice Wright until 2 p.m., when in fact she had been found dead at 1 p.m. The medical examination of Alice Wright showed she had been strangled.

The scene at the cottage was examined by the Police. A terrible fight appeared to have taken place, furniture having been knocked over and crockery broken and lying on the floor.

The Police later arrested John Harrison on suspicion of the murder of his wife Alice. On being searched he was found to be in possession of a purse belonging to Alice.

He was medically examined and his hands and clothing were found to be covered in blood.

Police enquiries about the antecedents of the couple showed that things were not as rosy as they would have people believe.

The pair were known to argue violently and frequently. The day before they had been seen in a violent argument on the highway leading up to the cottage.

Even though Harrison denied murdering Alice, and all the evidence against him was circumstantial, he was charged that he had wilfully and maliciously murdered Alice Ann Wright.

John Harrison was tried at Liverpool Assizes Court, St George's Hall, the trial being presided over by Mr Justice Bucknill.

During the trial Harrison remained calm, protesting his innocence throughout. The jury retired for one hour and twenty minutes before returning with a guilty verdict.

Harrison seemed stunned by the verdict, evidently expecting to be found innocent of the crime.

Mr Justice Bucknill put on the black cap and sentenced Harrison to death.

He was then conveyed to Walton Prison to await his execution.

During his time in prison, Harrison continued to protest his innocence; friends and family who visited him spread the word that he was innocent of the crime.

People around the country wondered whether perhaps an innocent man was about to be executed, miscarriages of justice being mentioned whenever people talked about the case.

Efforts were made by his legal representative to obtain a reprieve, but the Home Secretary having read the reports of the case decided that he couldn't alter the decision that had been reached by the court.

Harrison who had been quite buoyant up to this point,

now took on a mood of despair and he soon resigned himself to his fate.

On 23rd December, 1901, the condemned man was visited by the Governor of the Prison, Captain Henry Talbot Price, who spoke to Harrison for a short time and asked Harrison if he had anything to say to him. Harrison replied "No, only that I am guilty of the crime for which I am committed".

Later that evening William Billington arrived at the Prison with his brother Thomas. Both were the sons of the late James Billington who had been executioner at the prison on a number of occasions. Both sons had taken the baton from their father and had become executioners.

William Billington would carry out this execution assisted by his brother Thomas.

At 6.30 a.m. on 24th December, 1901, James Harrison woke to begin the last day of his life on earth, having spent a restless night in the condemned cell.

After a light breakfast he was joined by the Prison Chaplain, the Rev Morris, who led him in prayer for some time. The two Prison Officers who had spent the night looking over Harrison sat nearby.

At 7.55 a.m. William Billington accompanied by his brother Thomas came to the cell. Harrison was pinioned and led to the execution chamber.

He stood quietly whilst the white hood and noose were put over his head, the executioner looked towards the gathered officials; Governor Price nodded his head. At this signal Billington sprung the trap door lever sending Harrison to his death.

Death was due to dislocation of the vertebrae, and was instantaneous.

The estimated drop used by the executioner was 6 feet.

At the inquest later held in the Prison, the Coroner said, because of certain suggestions that had been made about the case, it was always a source of satisfaction, when a man confessed his guilt, which relieved those who had tried him of any sense of responsibility that perhaps they might have done something wrong.

Footnote: Prior to an execution, the Prison Governor would produce for inspection by the executioner, the warrant of death, signed by the Judge who pronounced sentence on the condemned person.

# The Execution of Thomas Marshland

In July, 1901, Thomas Marshland, 21 years, a piecer in a cotton mill, and working in Oldham, met an attractive young lady named Elizabeth. The relationship quickly developed into a full blown romance.

Elizabeth's parents, both middle class, were not too happy about the fact that Elizabeth was prepared to settle for Marshland. She was three years younger than Marshland, he being her first boyfriend.

Her parents had hoped that she would find someone who could give her a better standard of living than Thomas Marshland could provide.

Elizabeth persuaded her parents that she was happy with Thomas, and wanted to marry him. Her parents relented and gave them their blessing.

In November that year the couple were married and moved into rooms with a friend of Elizabeth's, a lady named Mrs Lowe.

Thomas and Elizabeth were fine for the first few months, but soon Thomas started staying out after work, drinking with his workmates. Elizabeth was happy to play the housewife, but soon tired of Thomas coming home late.

Both soon started arguing over the way Thomas was now behaving and Thomas would often lose his temper and mistreat Elizabeth. The situation became so bad that Mrs Lowe was forced to ask the couple to find alternative accommodation.

Eventually they moved into a terraced house at No1, Horsedge-Fold, Oldham. The situation between the two never improved,Thomas continuing to mistreat Elizabeth.

On Easter Monday, 30th April, 1902, the arguing got so bad that Elizabeth left the house and returned to stay with Mrs Lowe. Thomas became obsessed over Elizabeth leaving home, and once again turned to drink.

The following Friday, Elizabeth returned home, hoping that her absence may have struck home with Thomas and that he may have changed his ways.

Thomas had changed; his moods had become blacker, because he resented the fact that Elizabeth had left him.

On 4th May, 1902, Thomas visited a local cutler's shop and purchased a razor. He immediately went home and confronted Elizabeth.

A struggle took place in which Thomas overpowered Elizabeth. During the struggle Thomas used the razor and inflicked a deep wound in her throat; Elizabeth bled to death.

Thomas sat down looking at the body of his unfortunate wife, now lying dead on the floor, and realized the serious consequences of his actions.

Thomas walked out of the house closing the front door behind him. A short distance away he saw Constable Conway of the Oldham Police Force.

He approached the Police Officer and told him of the murder of his wife. The Officer listened to the man who told his tale in a calm manner.

Constable Conway finding Marshland's story hard to believe decided to take him to the Police Station. Marshland again repeated the grim tale, and produced the house key, to allow the Police Officers to investigate the incident.

Constable Conway together with other Officers returned with Marshland to Horsedge-fold and upon entering the house, the Police Officers discovered the body of Elizabeth Marshland lying on the living room floor.

Her throat had been cut in a forceful manner and blood was still seeping from the dreadful wound, that had been inflicted upon the unfortunate lady.

The razor which had been used to commit the crime, was found in the kitchen.

Marshland was arrested and appeared before the next Magistrates court. He was committed to Liverpool Assizes Court for trial charged with the wilful murder of his wife. Thomas Marshland was remanded in custody to Walton Prison.

The dreadful circumstances of the crime shocked the people of Oldham who turned out in the hundreds to watch the funeral of the young woman.

The accused man appeared before Mr Justice Walton at Liverpool Assizes where he pleaded guilty to the crime. He was represented by Mr Reginald Harrison, who had taken the brief at the request of the Judge.

In view of the guilty plea, Mr Harrison had little to put to the jury, except that the accused had not been in the right frame of mind, and was therefore not responsible for his actions.

The jury retired to consider the verdict, and returned within thirty minutes. They found the defendant guilty of the wilful murder of his wife.

The sentence of death was passed upon Marshland, who walked from the dock quickly and without showing the slightest concern.

The condemned man was taken to Walton Prison to await the sentence of the law to take its course.

Whilst in prison Marshland never showed any remorse, only getting upset when his elderly mother visited him. At this time he broke down, sobbing uncontrollably. He regained his composure before his mother left, asking her to pray for him.

No efforts to obtain a reprieve were made on behalf of the convicted man.

Because the weather was particularly warm during his detention in the condemned cell, Marshland was allowed to exercise in the prison yard. He spent the time just leaning against the wall soaking up the sun.

The indifferent attitude of Marshland didn't sit well with the prison staff who were to watch over him, and only in the last days, did he appear to heed the words of the Prison Chaplain who had tried to guide him on what would be the last journey of his short, but eventful life.

At 6.30 a.m. on 20th May, 1902, Thomas Marshland was up and enjoying his last breakfast. The Prison Chaplain, the Rev Morris, entered the condemned cell and greeted Marshland who quickly pushed his plate aside.

Marshland during the last few days had suddenly realised that the only course of action he could now take was to make his peace with God. He had come to look forward to his meeting with the Chaplain, but this was to be his last appointment.

At 7.55 a.m. William Billington entered the cell with the Prison Governor, the pinioning of Marshland's arms was quickly done. The death procession was soon on its way. Marshland took great interest in his last walk across the prison yard.

When the execution room came into view, the scaffold could be seen by the condemned man walking towards it. Marshland kept up his steady pace. He stood on the trap door, the white hood was pulled over his face, followed by the noose which was fastened firmly around his neck.

He was then dispatched to his death, in accordance with the letter of the law. His body was left hanging for the statutory hour. The Prison Medical Officer pronounced him dead. The time from when Marshland left the condemned cell till he was hung was less than two minutes.

At the inquest later that day, the reason for death was given as dislocation of the neck, due to lawful hanging. Death was said to be instantaneous.

Footnote: On the day Thomas Marshland appeared at Liverpool Assizes Court, he was one of six men charged with Murder. He was the only one to be sentenced to death.

# The Executions of Gustav Rau and Willem Schmidt

On 12th May, 1903, one of the most infamous trials to be heard in a court of law began at St George's Hall, Liverpool.

People around the world were spellbound at the horrific details of the alleged crimes.

During the next few days three men would stand trial for murder and mutiny on the high seas.

The story of the British ship *Veronica* would be the topic of conversation throughout the country for the next few days whilst the court was in session.

The three men Otto Monsoon, 18 years, Gustav Rau, 28 years, and Willem Schmidt, 30 years, were charged that in December, 1902, on various dates, whilst aboard the British ship *Veronica*, on the high seas, did wilfully murder seven men, namely McLeod, Abrahamson, Shaw, Johansen, Bravo, Parson and Doran.

The men were also charged with having set fire to the ship, and having conspired together to murder the named men, who were Officers and crew of the ship *Veronica*.

The court clerk read an indictment in regard to the alleged murder of Shaw, Captain of the *Veronica*. This charge was proceeded with apart from the other charges. If this charge failed, the men would be charged with the other alleged offences.

A model of the ship *Veronica* was displayed in the court, for inspection if required.

The trial was presided over by Mr Justice Lawrance, and the Prosecution was conducted by Mr Tobin K.C and Mr Smith.

The three defendants who had pleaded not guilty to the charges were also represented by Council.

Mr Maxwell appeared on behalf of Rau, Mr Cuthbert Smith for Monsoon, and at the request of the Judge, Mr Aggs acted for Willem Schmidt.

Mr Tobin in opening the Prosecution case outlined the following facts.

In October, 1902, the British ship *Veronica* set sail from Ship Island in the Gulf of Mexico, bound for Montevideo, the ship being manned by a multi-national crew of twelve men.

On 20th December, 1902, the ship was deliberately set on fire whilst on the high seas, and abandoned. It was alleged by the Prosecution, that prior to the ship being set on fire, seven of the crew had been violently murdered.

Out of the remaining five crew members, three appeared before the court charged with these dreadful crimes and the last two crew members would appear as witnesses on behalf of the Crown.

Mr Tobin then told the court, that the issue the jury would have to decide was, were these three men, or any, and which of them, guilty of the murder of the Captain of the *Veronica*.

He also explained that it would also be necessary to consider the circumstances under which the remaining six members of the crew met their deaths.

It was a complicated case which would require the full attention of the jury. Witnesses may give different versions, it was up to the jury to decide if it was truthful, and therefore give verdicts according to the evidence.

The measurements of the *Veronica* were given as 186 feet

in length, and of 1000 registered tonnage. The *Veronica* at the time of the incident was carrying a cargo of lumber, timber was also stored on deck.

Mr Tobin stated that the first few weeks after the ship sailed, conditions appeared to be fine, but unfortunately after a while the three accused men showed that they resented the Officers. The resentment in the men grew like a cancer and led to mutiny and murder on board the *Veronica.*

The Police during their investigation could find no reason for the resentment of the men towards the Officers of the *Veronica*, but whatever it was, it led to the men being so worked up about their grievances that they were prepared to get rid of their Officers by foul means.

A discussion took place between the main participants in the crime, about what would happen when they reached port. Would anyone speak out and tell the truth of what had occurred?

Rau and Schmidt, the ringleaders in the plot set about convincing the other members to stick together.

They resolved to get rid of fellow members of the crew they could not trust, men of a different nationality to themselves, a Swedish man named Johansen and a coloured man named Alex Bravo were to be amongst the murdered men.

The main players in the plot were of German origin, a fourth German crew member named Flohr, 18 years, joined in the conversation. Flohr was horrified when he was asked to join in the plot and when he told them he couldn't kill anyone Rau had told him, "You can choose between joining us, or going overboard."

Flohr at this point was persuaded to join with the other three Germans in carrying out the plot to take over the ship.

A plan was then drawn up by the conspirators in which they decided to pick off the Officers and crew, one by one during the night watch.

Paddy Doran was on watch that night and he would be the first to go. Flohr was told by Rau that he should deal with Doran but Flohr couldn't do the dirty deed.

Rau at this point walked up to Doran, and having armed himself with a knife and a heavy belaying pin, he engaged Doran in conversation, and when he had the opportunity he suddenly struck the unfortunate man two blows to the back of his head, knocking him unconscious. The injured man was thrown into a deck locker and was later thrown overboard.

Just then the first mate happened to come on deck looking for Doran and when he turned away from Rau, he was hit over the head and knocked unconscious. Two of the men then threw the unconscious first mate overboard.

Rau and Schmidt then armed themselves with revolvers that Rau had purchased on Ship Island and smuggled on board the *Veronica* with the intention of killing the Captain and Officers.

Monsoon was ordered to watch the Swedish seaman Johansen and the coloured man Bravo, making sure they couldn't warn anyone.

Rau and Schmidt now went towards the Officers quarters, shots were fired into the cabins. The second mate staggered wounded from his cabin and was taken prisoner.

Captain Shaw attempted to come on deck but was struck

with a belaying pin, and shot twice by Rau and fell back into his cabin badly wounded.

Rau then told Flohr to dispatch Johansen with a belaying pin. Johansen who had been at the steering wheel, was struck by Flohr. It was a glancing blow, and Johansen managed to run away to the other end of the ship, leaving no-one to steer the ship. Flohr at this point stayed at the steering wheel.

The Captain and the second mate were then barricaded in their cabins, and were kept imprisoned for several days without food or water.

The ship's cook, Moses Thomas, who had been asleep in his cabin woke up and discovered what was occurring, and at once locked himself in his cabin. Rau's threats made the cook open his door and give himself up.

Rau had the rest of the crew detained, whilst he and Schmidt decided what to do next.

After a few days, Rau found he was unable to sail the ship without charts and implements essential for navigation. He was now forced to barter with Captain Shaw for these articles.

Captain Shaw, although badly wounded, managed to obtain water for the second mate and himself.

The leaders of the mutiny held a council of war and decided it would be better if both Captain Shaw and the second mate were dead.

Rau, Schmidt and Monsoon had revolvers and Flohr stood nearby. They ordered the second mate to come out from his cabin and when he saw the heavily armed men he turned and attempted to return to his cabin.

Schmidt immediately shot him in the back, the force of

the bullet knocking him over the side of the ship into the water. Although badly wounded he attempted to swim away from the ship; the three armed men fired their revolvers at him and he sank beneath the water.

Just then the Captain staggered from his cabin, his hands held up in front of his face. He pleaded for his life but Rau walked towards the wounded man and shot him in the head.

The men then decided to set fire to the ship, so as no trace of the crime would be found.

They concocted a tale in which the ship caught fire, the crew had escaped in two lifeboats and they intended to tell whoever rescued them that the remainder of the crew were in the other lifeboat, and they must have perished

Seven of the crew now remained on the *Veronica*, the dead men's bodies having been thrown overboard. Rau now told the remaining crew members to commit the story of the ship catching fire to memory.

The Swedish seaman Johansen and Alex Bravo couldn't get the story right. Rau had no messing about with them - they were both killed and thrown into the sea.

Rau now had a lifeboat prepared, provisions such as food and water were put on board, and the *Veronica* was set on fire using timber from the cargo over which oil was poured.

The five men sailed off in the lifeboat, Rau making sure that the men committed to memory the story of the accidental fire on board the *Veronica*.

After a few days the lifeboat finally reached an island named Cajueria. The island although uninhabited was on a main shipping route, vessels would often call at the island and exchange cargoes.

The day after the five men landed on the Island, a British ship, the *Brunswick* arrived at the Island. Rau and the cook, Moses Thomas, rowed out to the *Brunswick*, and once on board the ship Rau told the story of the *Veronica* accidentally catching fire.

The few men were invited to remain on the *Brunswick* which was on route to Liverpool via Lisbon.

On board the *Brunswick*, the cook, Moses Thomas, had at his own request, asked to be kept apart from the other four men.

During the voyage to Lisbon, Moses requested an interview with the Captain of the *Brunswick*, during which he told the story of the murders and destruction of the *Veronica*.

When the ship reached Lisbon the crew of the *Veronica* were not allowed ashore. The ship then sailed to Liverpool, where the Police were informed of the fate of the *Veronica*. The five men were arrested on suspicion of murder and remained in custody whilst Police enquiries continued.

Within hours the German members of the *Veronica* crew now changed their story. They now blamed the cook, Moses Thomas, saying it was him, armed with a revolver and belaying pins who had murdered the men and set the ship on fire.

Flohr at this point realising how bad the situation was, asked to make a statement regarding the incident.

Flohr's statement corroborated  the statement that the cook had given to the Captain of the *Brunswick*.

The Crown therefore decided to withdraw the charges against Flohr and use him as a prosecution witness along with the cook.

During the trial Flohr gave evidence to the court that Rau had approached him weeks before the murders and had asked him to join with them. Flohr had refused and had been threatened by Rau into joining with them.

During his evidence, he told the full story of the conspiracy by Rau, Schmidt and Monsoon to take over the *Veronica*, to kill the Officers and burn the ship. He gave details of each man's part in the dreadful deed.

He was able to confirm that the cook, Moses Thomas had taken no part in the murders or the burning of the ship.

His description of the deaths of Johansen and Alex Bravo brought gasps of horror from the court. He described how Johansen was shot by Rau, and then shot in the head by Schmidt, his body was then thrown overboard.

Alex Bravo was fired upon, but managed to escape by jumping overboard. Rau now shot at the man in the water, and his body sank beneath the waves.

Although he was sternly cross-examined by the defence Barristers, he stuck firmly to the tale he had told the court.

Moses Thomas gave evidence next and his story corroborated the story told by Flohr.

William Watson, Chief Officer of the ship *Brunswick*, told the court of meeting Rau at Cajueria Island after the *Veronica* had been burnt and sunk. Rau had claimed to be the second mate from the *Veronica* and had told of the accidental fire on the *Veronica*.

He had claimed the Captain had been killed after falling off the fore top sail.

The Captain of the *Brunswick*, George Brown, during his evidence told the court of the tale Moses Thomas had told him, about the murders and destruction of the *Veronica*. During his evidence he described how he had kept a careful watch over the men and explained his decision not to allow the men ashore in Lisbon.

He had contacted the British Consul whilst in Lisbon and had made him aware of the allegations that had been made by Moses Thomas. The Police in England were told of the situation and had been waiting in Liverpool for the arrival of the *Brunswick*.

When the ship had docked at Liverpool, he identified the five men to the Police, who had then arrested them.

Other crewmen from the *Brunswick* were called to give evidence, they recounted stories, that the crew of the *Veronica* had told them regarding the fire and that Rau had claimed to be the second mate,from the *Veronica*.

The Police Officers then gave evidence of the arrest and interviews with the defendants.

When the defence came to present their evidence Rau was called first. He denied being involved in any of the murders,and placed all the blame on the cook, Moses Thomas, stating that the cook had a revolver, and along with Flohr, was responsible for all the trouble on the *Veronica*.

Willem Schmidt was next to give evidence, and he also blamed Moses Thomas for the murders. He went on to say that Rau had been placed in charge of the ship by Moses after the Officers had been shot. He denied being responsible for any of the deaths or of setting the ship on fire.

Monsoon did not take the stand to give his version of events on the *Veronica*.

Mr Tobin in summing up for the prosecution laid the blame firmly on the three defendants. He claimed the defence were unable to disprove certain true facts. Seven men had been killed out of a crew of twelve in the most violent of ways.

The defendants had travelled some thousands of miles from the scene of the murderous incident, and had only spoke of the crime after their arrest.

He told the jury that the story of the *Veronica* would not have come out if Moses Thomas had not requested to speak with the Captain of the *Brunswick*. The later statement made by Flohr corroborated the tale told by Moses Thomas.

This statement by Flohr was made without him knowing that Thomas had already spoken to Captain Brown of the *Brunswick.*

At the conclusion of his summing up, Mr Tobin asked the jury to say that each of the prisoners was alike guilty of the crime of murder.

Mr Maxwell speaking on behalf of Rau, pointed out that Flohr instead of giving evidence against the defendants should be in the dock with them. He claimed Flohr's evidence was entirely unworthy of belief. He also threw the blame for the murders upon the cook Moses Thomas.

Mr Cuthbert Smith representing Monsoon stated that the prosecution had failed in putting forward a case against Monsoon. It was not for Monsoon to prove he was innocent, it was for the prosecution to prove him guilty. This was the reason why Monsoon had not been called to give evidence.

He asked the jury to discount the evidence given by Moses

Thomas, and attacked Flohr calling him an informer, when he was in fact a self-confessed liar. He said Flohr was an untrustworthy witness, and had been an active participant in all that had taken place.

On behalf of Monsoon, he was not asking for mercy, he was asking the court for justice.

Mr Aggs for the defendant Schmidt claimed the inconsistencies in the prosecution were in fact lies told by the main witnesses Thomas and Flohr. He claimed the evidence given by Schmidt was consistent in its detail, and was truthful.

His Lordship Mr Justice Lawrance in summing up said that it was not necessary that the prosecution should prove that each of the three men did some personal violence to Captain Shaw, the main question was, were the men acting in concert with a common purpose.

The jury retired to consider their verdict, they returned within fifteen minutes, and were formally asked by the Clerk of the Court if they had reached a verdict.

The Foreman of the jury said that they had found the prisoners guilty of murder and he added that the jury wished Monsoon to be recommend for mercy on account of his youth and previous good character.

Mr Justice Lawrance in addressing the prisoners said the jury had found the men guilty of the murder on the evidence that had been presented to them.

He told Monsoon that the recommendation of the jury would be past to the proper quarters in due course.

He then pronounced sentence of death upon the three men, who betrayed no sign of agitation, and walked calmly from the dock.

The men were later transported to Walton Prison to await the date of their execution.

Monsoon was later reprieved following the jury's recommendation of mercy, and sentenced to penal servitude for life.

During their time in Walton prison, the two condemned men Rau and Schmidt were kept in separate cells.

Both men were visited by German Pastors. The men seemed indifferent to anyone who came into contact with them.

The executioners William Billington and his brother Thomas arrived on the evening of 1st June, 1903. During the evening they visited the men in the condemned cell.

The following morning, the day of the execution, both men rose early and had breakfast. They showed no signs of fear of the terrible fate that awaited them.

A large number of people took up position in Hornby Road outside the Prison, looking towards the Prison tower for the raising of the black flag.

Both men when the time came for them to be pinioned offered not the slightest resistance; they had not seen each other since arriving at the Prison, but now nodded to each other, both resigned to their fate.

The procession moved quickly to the execution chamber, both condemned men were placed on the trap door. The Billingtons moved quickly around the scaffold, both men were now fully strapped ready for their execution.

Schmidt stood on the scaffold waiting to meet his doom, Rau had his death hood pulled over his head, the rope was pulled over his head and adjusted around his neck. Just then he turned towards the Prison Governor and said " I am innocent of the deaths of those men."

Before he could utter another word, Billington pulled the trap door lever and both men fell to their death.

At the Coroners Court which was held later that morning, the Coroner having received a verdict from the jury, remarked this was the end of a terrible tragic episode.

# The Execution of
# Henry Bertram Starr

On 24th, November, 1903, the people of the Lancashire seaside resort of Blackpool were shocked at the vicious murder of a young married mother who lived in the town.

The victim of this crime was Mary Hannah Starr, the perpetrator being her estranged husband, Henry Bertram Starr, who would pay the ultimate penalty for the unwarranted attack upon his wife which had resulted in her death.

The story of their relationship began some twelve months earlier, when Henry Starr, who lived in Blackpool with his auntie, Mrs Warren, called on the Blagg family who resided a few streets away.

Starr introduced himself to the Blagg family as a possible suitor for their daughter Mary.

Mary a pretty girl had seen Starr about the district, and was impressed by his good looks and confident nature.

The family agreed to Starr's request to court Mary, and were quickly won over by his easy going ways. Within a week or so, Starr had moved in with the Blagg family.

The relationship quickly developed, and in March, 1903, the couple married. They continued to live with Mary's family and everything seemed to be fine between Henry and Mary.

Towards the end of June the marriage came under some strain. Henry started drinking a lot, his behaviour towards Mary changed and he became violent.

He began to have terrible mood swings, and as a result he and his wife parted. Henry returned to live with his aunt, Mrs Warren.

Henry occasionally visited Mary, but did himself no favours when in August, he told her he had been unfaithful to her. Mary later wrote to Starr and told him never to come near her again.

On 21st August, 1903, a child was born to Mary. Henry renewed his relationship with Mary, and returned to live with her.

After a few months, Starr returned to his drunken and violent ways and Mary realized things were no better, told him the marriage was over and Starr again returned to live with his aunt.

Henry Starr then wrote to Mary stating that if she was not prepared to live with him, he would seek custody of the child.

Mary in response to his threats took a summons out against him. On 23rd November, 1903, he was ordered by the Magistrates to pay six shillings a week maintenance to his wife. Starr was livid at the thought Mary had taken him to court and had been awarded the sum of six shillings a week.

The same evening Starr was seen out drinking in a number of public houses. During the evening he seemed to have worked himself up into a frenzy, and was determined to do some harm to Mary.

After having some five or six pints of beer, he made his way to the house where his wife was living with her mother.

Near to the house, a coachman saw him talking to himself, and he was overheard repeating the words "I'll do it, I'll do it".

At 8 a.m. on 24th November, 1903 Mary Starr was up and about the house doing breakfast.

She opened the kitchen door leading to the back yard, when suddenly Henry Starr who had been hiding in the yard from the previous evening rushed at her holding a bread knife.

Starr began a savage attack upon the unfortunate woman, hacking at Mary's face and body. Mary managed to scream for help before the horrific attack forced her to the ground. Her mother Mrs Blagg came running into the kitchen, and saw Henry Starr standing over her daughter plunging the knife into her.

Starr on being discovered by Mrs Blagg, escaped from the house through the back yard, leaving his wife lying mortally wounded in a pool of blood.

A doctor was called to the house and pronounced Mary dead, there were ten stab wounds on her neck and body. Some wounds were on her arms where she had attempted to defend herself.

In her breast was a wound, so deep and wide, the Doctor could put his fist into it.

The Police were called to the scene of the murder, and immediately commenced a search for Henry Starr. They discovered that he had called at two hotels, where he had ordered drinks and the bar staff had noticed his hands were covered in blood.

Police finally traced him to a public toilet in Talbot Street, where he was attempting to wash the blood of his victim from his hands. When he was arrested for the crime, he asked the arresting Officer " Is she dead ?" .

He was taken to the Police station, and later charged with the wilful and malicious murder of Mary Hannah Starr.

He appeared at Blackpool Magistrates Court the following day, and was committed for trial at Liverpool Assizes Court.

In December, 1903, Henry Starr appeared at Liverpool Assizes Court, St Georges Hall, where he pleaded not guilty to the offence.

The trial was presided over by Mr Justice Ridley, Mr Madden represented the defendant Starr.

Mr Madden called no witnesses for the defence but he put forward the submission that, at the time of the attack, Starr was not in his right mind. He didn't deny that Starr had inflicted the wounds, but he asked the jury to conclude that Starr was in a disordered mental condition as to be incapable of a complete unqualified intent, that would justify them bringing in a verdict of guilty. In short, Starr had killed his wife whilst under the influence of alcohol.

The jury disagreed with this argument, and without leaving the court, brought in a verdict of guilty.

Starr who had appeared indifferent throughout the proceedings was taken to Walton Prison to await his fate.

Many people who had followed the progress of the case, believed the verdict to be a true reflection of the crime.

During his incarceration at Walton Prison, Henry Starr displayed a demeanour of couldn't care less attitude for the predicament he now found himself in.

Normally when a person is sentenced to death, someone would get up a petition in order to obtain a reprieve for the condemned man. In this case, no attempt was made to stop the execution; many people thought he should die for the horrendous crime.

On Saturday, 26th December, 1903, any lingering hope that Starr may have held were dashed when correspondence was received at the prison that the law must take its course.

This information was conveyed to Starr, when he was visited by his Solicitor later that day.

Whilst in prison, Starr had few visitors. He did however looked forward to his visits from the Prison Chaplain, the Reverend Morris, who passed many hours with the condemned man.

Executioner William Billington arrived the previous evening with his assistant Henry Albert Pierpoint, who was to watch the proceedings as part of his training. Billington and Pierpoint were met by the Deputy Governor of the Prison, Walter Kelly.

The morning of the execution saw Starr up and about the condemned cell at an early hour, his last night on earth being one in which he had little sleep.

When the time came for the final act of the law to be carried out, Starr displayed no fear and stood quite still whilst the executioner went about his duties.

On the stroke of 8 a.m. Billington completed his job by pulling the trap door lever and sending Starr to his death.

The drop given by Billington at the inquest held later at the prison was 6ft - 10 inches. Death was instantaneous.

Few people had gathered outside the prison on this cold and dark morning. The routine of displaying the black flag after an execution had been abolished some weeks earlier.

The grim sound of the chiming prison clock gave the only clue, that the condemned man had met his fate.

The usual notices were pinned to the prison main gate confirming the execution had been carried out.

Footnote: The murder of his wife at Blackpool was the second capital offence for which Henry Bertram Starr was tried.

On 24th April, 1896 he was tried at the Manchester Assizes for the murder of his sweetheart, Eleanor Coulthart, by drowning her in the River Ribble.

The defence was that the girl's death was due to either suicide, or an execution. The slenderness of the evidence, and his demeanour, when being told of the death of his sweetheart was played on by his Barrister. Starr was found not guilty by the jury and was discharged.

# The Execution of William Kirwan

On 26th February, 1904, an incident occurred in Liverpool that became known as the Great Newton Street tragedy.

The incident resulted in the death of two people, the first the victim, Mary Pike, 25 years, and her brother-in-law, William Kirwan, 39 years, who was later executed for her murder.

The circumstances of the crime relate to the unfaithfulness of a married woman.

William Kirwan, a sailor by profession, was married to his wife Katie for some thirteen years, the couple had two children by the marriage.

In February, 1904, William Kirwan returned home after a trip abroad. At first everything at home appeared to be normal, but after a week or so, he thought his wife's behaviour towards him had changed, she didn't seem to be as affectionate as she had been.

Katie also seemed to be spending more time than she normally did at her sister's home at 31, Great Newton Street, Liverpool. Her sister Mary Pike was also married to a sailor named Sydney John Pike.

William just thought that being sisters, with their husbands being away a lot of the time, the sisters had grown closer, confiding in one another.

At 4 p.m. on 26th February, 1904, Katie had left the family home at Richmond Row, Liverpool, taking her children to visit Mary.

William Kirwan left alone in the house somehow discovered a letter from a man addressed to his wife. The letter told of the man's feelings for Katie, and of the time they had spent together at Mary's house.

Kirwan at once armed himself with a revolver, and went in search of Katie, who by now had reached her sister's house.

When Kirwan reached 31, Great Newton Street, he found Katie and Mary talking together. He at once accused Katie

*Outside Walton Prison 1900s*
*Courtesy of Liverpool Record Office*

of being unfaithful, and Mary of letting the affair take place in her house.

Both women denied this had taken place. Kirwan told them of the letter he had found, which was proof of what had occurred behind his back.

The argument grew more heated, suddenly Kirwan pulled the revolver from his pocket and fired a number of shots at Katie. Mary Pike ran into the hallway followed by Kirwan,. Just then a man named Russell who rented rooms upstairs came downstairs. Mary Pike shouted to him that Katie had been shot in the parlour.

Mr Russell saw that Kirwan had a revolver in his hand pointing it towards Mary Pike. He at once put himself in front of Mary Pike, and opened the door to the parlour. He could see Katie standing there, she appeared to be wounded.

He pulled Katie out of the room and placing himself between both women moved them along the passage towards the back of the house.

With both women apparently safe, he moved towards William Kirwan and managed to push him out of the house, locking the front door behind him.

Mrs Russell upon hearing the noise, looked out of an upstairs window and saw Kirwan standing on the steps reloading the revolver.

William Kirwan suddenly walked off towards Pembroke Place, firing the revolver into the air.

A short distance away he met a man named Teare, and complained to him about his wife's conduct, he also told him that the house at 31, Great Newton Street was one in which disorderly conduct took place.

Just then a Police Officer who had seen Kirwan discharging the firearm in the street took hold of him, and detained him.

Mary Pike on seeing the Police Officer detain Kirwan, came out of her house and walked towards them, shouting to the Police Officer that Kirwan had shot his Wife.

Kirwan on seeing Mary pulled the revolver from his pocket and fired the gun at her, the bullet struck Mary Pike in the side, she fell wounded to the ground.

Mary Pike was taken to the Royal Infirmary with a wound to her left side, despite medical treatment she succumbed to her injuries and died on Friday, 4th March, 1904.

Kirwan was taken to the local Police Station and detained whilst enquiries into the incident was made by Detectives. Kirwan was interviewed regarding the shooting when he told the interviewing Police Officers that he intended to kill the pair of them, he was sorry he did not.

After Mary died, William Kirwan was charged with her murder, he was remanded in custody to appear before Liverpool Assizes Court.

On 9th, May, 1904, William Kirwan appeared before Liverpool Spring Assizes Court, and was indicted for the wilful murder of Mary Pike.

The court was presided over by Mr Justice Bucknall, the Prosecution was conducted by Mr Maxwell and Mr Segar. The defendant was represented by Mr Madden.

The first witness to be called was Sydney Pike, the husband of the deceased lady. He told the court that he had counted four bullet marks on the parlour walls.

A statement taken from Mary Pike in the Royal Infirmary was read to the court in which she described the incident which led to her being shot. She denied that Katie had been unfaithful to her husband in her house. She stated that Kirwan had fired two shots at his wife, and two shots at her, none of the shots had struck home, until she had gone outside.

John Russell, a Cotton Porter, was next into the witness box, he was the man who had placed himself between the gunman and the women.

During his evidence Russell told the court that he was coming downstairs when he heard the shots, Mary Pike had come into the hallway, he saw William Kirwan standing with a revolver pointed at Mary. She had told him Katie was in the parlour.

He went to the parlour and forced open the door, Katie ran to him and sheltered behind him, he moved back into the hallway and placed himself between Kirwan and the two women, Mary's children were with her, he then ushered them down the passage and into the cellar, closing the door behind them.

He next turned towards Kirwan who had remained standing at the bottom of the stairs, he moved towards Kirwan who had backed towards the front door. When they reached the doorway, Russell pushed Kirwan into the street and locked the door behind him.

After a few minutes he opened the front door and saw a Police Constable take hold of William Kirwan. Just then Mary Pike had come up from the cellar to see what was happening and upon seeing the Police Officer with Kirwan she left the safety of the house and went towards them.

Kirwan seeing Mary approach them pulled out the revolver and shot her from a distance of three yards.

The man named Teare who Kirwan had spoken to some minutes prior to the shooting gave evidence to the effect that he had assisted the Constable to detain Kirwan and remove him to the Police Station.

The arresting Police Officer told the court that he had detained Kirwan and asked him for the revolver. Kirwan suddenly drew the firearm and fired it at Mary Pike who had approached from behind the Constable.

At the Police Station, he had charged Kirwan with the attempted murder of his wife, Catherine Kirwan and Mary Pike.

After the death of Mary Pike he had charged Kirwan with the wilful murder of the woman. Kirwan had replied " I have nothing to say, only that I have been driven to it with great provocation ".

Dr Knowles from the Royal Infirmary confirmed that Mary Pike had been admitted to hospital with a bullet wound to the left side which had fractured a rib on the right side. Septic Poisoning had set in, and the woman had died on 4th,March, 1904.

Mr Madden in opening the defence called Katie Kirwan to give evidence. It was put to her about being unfaithful to her husband, she denied this. When asked about the letter her husband had found, she denied seeing it until produced by her husband.

William Kirwan was next to give evidence. He explained about finding the letter in his wife's bed, and going to the Pike's house. He had asked Mary Pike about the details given in the letter, she had confirmed it.

When he had challenged his wife Katie, she had denied it. At this point he pulled the revolver from his pocket and fired at both women, but missing them.

He had left the house and spoken to the man named Teare when the Police Constable came up, detained him and asked him for the revolver. Just then Mary Pike came out from the house and started calling him foul names. He took the revolver from his pocket and shot her, he then handed the firearm to the Constable.

Mr Madden in summing up for the defence, told the jury, he could not put forward seriously that the prisoner was insane, but many minds not absolutely insane were disordered and without proper balance. One of the things that turned a man's mind was some wrong, real or fancied, and if there was one passion more than another, in the palace or the slums, which disordered the mind it was the jealousy which spring up almost irresistibly in the mind of a man who believed his wife had been unfaithful. Would any man who was not a madman or a fool shoot his victim when the hand of the law was upon him.

His Lordship summed up and he said that the prisoner had admitted that he shot the deceased woman, and he shot her intentionally. He further admitted that he had done it after what had gone before solely because she had called him certain foul names. There could be no other verdict than a verdict of murder.

The jury without leaving the court returned a verdict of guilty of wilful murder.

His Lordship assumed the black cap, and addressing the prisoner, his Lordship said on the clearest possible evidence he had been found guilty of the murder of Mary Pike. His Lordship told him he believed then and now his wife had been unfaithful to him but this did not excuse him taking a life of the woman even if she had known of the infidelity, if she ever did. He had the courage to stand up and own up to the crime. He implored him to spend what little time he had left and make his peace with his maker.

His Lordship then passed sentence of death upon William Kirwan.

The prisoner received the sentence with the same firmness in the end as he had throughout the proceedings.

The prisoner was conveyed to Walton Prison to await the sentence of the law to be carried out.

During the next few weeks a petition for a reprieve was sent to the Home Secretary on behalf of Kirwan.

On 27th May, 1904, correspondence was received from the Home Office stating that after reading the notes of the case, the Home Secretary is unable to interfere with the sentence of death passed by the court.

At 8a.m on 31st May, 1904, William Kirwan was executed at Walton Prison, Liverpool. The executioner was William Billington.

Footnote: Also executed with William Kirwan was a Chinese man named Pong Lun, this was the second double execution at the Prison

*Great Newton Street present day*

# The Execution of Pong Lun

At 8 a.m. on Tuesday, 31st May, 1904, a Chinese man named Pong Lun joined William Kirwan in the execution chamber at Walton Prison, Liverpool.

Both men who had never met before found themselves standing next to each other on the gallows.

The men had been convicted of murder, Kirwan of murdering his sister-in-law, Mary Pike, and Pong Lun of murdering his friend John Go-Hing.

The condemned men had used firearms to commit the crimes, and now both were to pay the ultimate price, the loss of their own lives.

William Kirwan was first to be placed on the scaffold, the death mask was pulled over his head, and the noose adjusted around his neck. Pong Lun had followed Kirwan into the execution chamber, he stood quietly on the scaffold watching the proceeding. He had held his nerve up to this stage, but now he started to shake involuntary.

William Billington, the executioner was assisted by Henry Pierpoint, he had done his duty many times, and was confident that all would be well on this occasion.

He saw that Pong Lun was becoming distressed and quickly moved to deal with him. He guided Lun onto the chalk mark that had been drawn onto the wooden trap door.

Billington soon had Pong Lun pinioned about the legs, he could see that Lun had now regained his posture. The mask was pulled over his head, and the rope fastened in place. Both men stood erect, as though bracing themselves for the ordeal to come. Billington glanced at the Prison

Governor who signalled for the execution to proceed. With a smooth movement the lever was pulled, the trap door opened and both men dropped to their deaths.

The bodies both remained hanging for the statutory hour, before being moved to the Prison Hospital Mortuary, where both bodies would be viewed by the Coroners jury. Both men would later be buried in the same grave.

Kirwan had killed because of jealousy, Pong Lun had killed because of his gambling habits.

The story of how Pong Lun came to his violent end, was one in which many Chinese participate, the game of Chinese dominoes, Mah Jong.

At 8 p.m. on Sunday, 20th, March, 1904, Pong Lun, 43 years, a store man was at 22a, Frederick Street, Liverpool, the premises being a lodging house frequented by Chinese men. Other men at the premises included his friend and work colleague John Go-Hing from Rock Ferry.

John Go-Hing ran a Laundry in Birkenhead, but often travelled to Liverpool and met up with his countrymen in the Chinatown area of Liverpool.

The game of Mah Jong was in progress, Pong Lun was watching the game and he wanted to bet on the hand of one of the players. This could only happen with the permission of the banker. John Ho-Hing was the banker at the time, he refused to accept the bet of Pong Lun who had placed his money on the table.

The player Pong Lun had wanted to back won the hand, John Ho-Hing refused to pay Pong Lun telling him he had refused the bet. Pong Lun became angry and stormed out of the room.

He returned to the room a short time later holding a revolver and he fired two shots at John Ho-Hing, who fell to the floor shouting Pong Lun has shot me.

With that Pong Lun ran from the room and left the house firing his gun into the air, to deter anyone from following him.

The Police were called to the scene, and a search of the area recovered a revolver which was later confirmed as being the murder weapon.

John Ho-Hing was taken to the Northern Hospital with a wound to his stomach, he failed to recover from the injury and died three days later. Pong Lun had fled from the scene, but returned to the house the following morning and was arrested by the Police. He told the Officers that Ho-Hing owed him money, and had refused to pay him.

Pong Lun was later charged with the wilful murder of his friend. On 9th May, 1904, he appeared before Mr Justice Bucknall at Liverpool Spring Assizes Court and was defended by Mr Madden.

Witnesses were called to say that on the night of the shooting, Pong Lun was quite drunk; normally he was a man of a quiet nature who drank very little.

Mr Madden didn't call Pong Lun to give evidence as he only spoke in pigeon English. He urged the jury to consider that Pong Lun was drunk when he killed his friend and it was an action he would never have taken had he been sober. He asked the jury to return a verdict of Manslaughter against his client.

The jury having listened to the evidence returned a verdict of guilty to the murder of John Ho-Hing.

Mr Justice Bucknall in passing sentence of death, remarked he had been found guilty on the clearest evidence of the crime, of murder of a man who was apparently his friend up to almost the last moment.

*Frederick Street*

Pong Lun was removed to Walton Prison, he had few visitors whilst waiting fore the sentence of the court to be carried out.

Efforts were made to obtain a reprieve on behalf of Pong Lun by the Liverpool Branch for the abolition of Capital Punishment. The Home Secretary refused to alter the sentence that had been imposed by the court.

On 31st May, 1904, Pong Lun went to his death with William Kirwan.

The Coroners Court later returned verdicts that death was due to dislocation of the vertebrae of the neck, death was instantaneous for both men.

# The Execution of Charles Patterson

One of the quickest murder trials in history took place in July, 1907, at  St Georges Hall, Liverpool.

The defendant Charles Patterson, 31 years, a sailor had been arrested in Moss Side, Manchester for the murder of his common law wife.

Patterson, a heavy set man from Jamaica, had arrived in Salford Docks some twelve months earlier when his ship arrived from the West Indies. When his ship sailed a few days later, Patterson was not aboard, he had decided to stay in Salford and look for work ashore.

Apart from the odd days work around the docks, Patterson couldn't find regular employment. He then decided to move to the Moss Side area of Manchester.

He was given accommodation by various friends he made in the local clubs and public houses. After a time he seemed to spend more time  drinking than working and any money he made was soon spent.

In July, 1906, he became involved with a woman named Lillian Jane Charlton who had been apart from her husband for a number of years.

Lillian had four children from her marriage, two of the children still living at home with her in Moss Side.

The relationship was a stormy affair, Patterson now did little or no work. Lillian would give him money which he told her was to help him travel around looking for work. More often than not he would end up coming home drunk.

On Saturday evening, 29th June, 1907, Patterson again arrived home the worse for drink. Lillian was in the kitchen talking with her daughter and no sooner had Patterson walked into the room, when Lillian said to him " Enough is enough - what a fool I am - to think I should have lowered myself through a man like you " .

I have kept you for twelve months, and not a penny have I had from you. You should be ashamed of yourself, what will I do for food on Sunday."

Lillian then stormed out of the room, slamming the door behind her and went upstairs.

No sooner had she left the room, when Patterson followed her, running upstairs behind her. Within minutes terrible screams were heard coming from the bathroom of the house.

Lillian's son George, who had been visiting his mother rushed upstairs and met Patterson coming down, " I have done it " Patterson said to George.

Her son went into the bathroom and saw his mother lying dead on the floor, her throat had been cut from ear to ear. Charles Patterson's razor was by her side.

The Police were summoned to the scene, and Charles Patterson was arrested for the murder of Lillian Charlton.

He was later interviewed at the Police Station and when asked for the reason for his attacking the deceased, he replied "It was my temper, I have had my revenge" .

He was later charged with her murder, and the following Monday, he appeared at the local Magistrates Court. He was remanded in custody to appear before Liverpool Assizes Court.

On Tuesday, 16th July, 1907, Patterson appeared before Mr Justice Channell at Liverpool Assizes Court, St Georges Hall, Liverpool. The Clerk of the Court read out the charge of murder against Patterson, who replied "Guilty" in a loud and clear voice.

His Lordship explained to the prisoner, that the charge was murder, not manslaughter, he then explained the implications of the plea.

He concluded by asking Patterson if he understood the charge. Patterson replied "I quite understand it, sir".

His Lordship then asked if the Doctor from Walton Prison was present, and could he come forward. Dr Price, the Prison Medical Officer entered the witness box and, on the instructions of the judge, questioned the prisoner as to his right frame of mind.

Patterson again said that he understood his position, but still wished to admit his guilt of the crime. Dr Price was able to tell the Court that he had made enquiries in Manchester, and the authorities had no reason to suspect the prisoner's sanity, and the prisoner from his observations was quite sane.

His Lordship although reluctant to accept the guilty plea, and having had further consultations as to the prisoner's condition, finally assumed the black cap, and passed sentence of death upon Patterson.

The Judge in concluding stated that he thought it right to make enquiries in this case, before accepting the prisoner's plea of guilty, in order to see, if possible, whether there might be any mitigating circumstances that could reduce the offence to one of manslaughter, or to show that the prisoner was not responsible for his actions at the time.

On Wednesday, 7th, August, 1907, correspondence was received at Walton Prison to the effect that the Home Secretary had decided not to interfere with the due course of the law, and so the execution would proceed.

Throughout his detention at Walton Prison Patterson remained indifferent to his predicament.

At 8 a.m. the same morning Charles Patterson was executed by Henry Albert Pierpoint.

The inquest that followed the execution recorded a verdict of death by hanging in accordance with the law.

# The Execution of See Lee

On Saturday, 27th March, 1909, members of the works department at Walton Prison, Liverpool, dug and prepared a grave in the grounds of the prison, the grave would be used the following Tuesday for the burial of a convicted murderer who would be executed that day.

The execution of See Lee on Tuesday, 30th March, 1909, would see a crowd of over two hundred people gather in Hornby Road, Liverpool.

The Liverpool branch for the abolition of Capital Punishment paraded with their banners outside the Prison gates.

Some Chinese men, believed to be friends of the condemned man, had arrived at 8.30 a.m. having travelled by train from Liverpool to Walton Junction. They stood quietly on the opposite side of the road to the prison, sharing perhaps a last thought of their friend.

The execution was to be at 9 a.m. Officials connected with the execution had started to arrive at the prison at 8.15 a.m. and gained entrance to the premises.

Now that the black flag had ceased to be used to signal that the execution had taken place, the crowd listened for the prison clock to chime. They knew that once the last chime had sounded the condemned man would have met his fate.

Some time later the notice of death was pinned to the prison gate signed by the Under Sherriff of Lancashire, Mr T. E. Wilson, confirming the execution had taken place in accordance with the sentence of the law.

The story that brought See Lee to such a dreadful fate was one that had been around since time began, one man's jealousy against another, over the affections of a woman.

Some twelve months earlier, See Lee, a seaman resided in lodgings off Frederick Street, Liverpool, the area known as Chinatown. He became friendly with a lady named Amy Yap Sing (Amy was an English woman, who was married to a Chinese man who had since returned to China).

Amy lived in rooms in Dickenson Street, Liverpool. She had been ill for some months, and was now confined to bed.

See Lee would often call at the house to see her and he would often meet another Chinese man named Yung Yap, who was also a friend of the lady, and would also visit her at her rooms.

The two men appeared to get on well together, both concerned for Amy during her illness.

See Lee had over the months become very fond of Amy, but would never let his feeling be known to his fellow suitor.

Both men were often seen in the streets around Chinatown talking to each other, people who saw then believed them to be friends, but this was not the case.

The matter was also complicated by the fact that both men were members of different triads that existed in China-town at that time.

At 9 p.m. on Saturday, 4th December, 1908, See Lee called at Dickenson Street, to see Amy Yap Sing. Her friend, Yung Yap, had arrived some minutes earlier and on hearing the sound of footsteps on the stairs, opened the door and looked out. He returned to the room and told her "It is Ah Yak" another name for See Lee.

Within seconds See Lee entered the room and fired a revolver at Yung Yap. The shot caused a wound in the side of Yung Yap and he fell across the bed in which Amy Yap Sing was lying.

Amy shouted at See Lee, " What have you done to poor old Sukie?" See Lee never replied but turned and walked out of the room and went downstairs.

On the way out of the premises, he passed a lady named Mrs Harris. He had often talked to her, but on this occasion, he just smiled at her and carried on walking.

The injured man Yung Yap managed to crawl from the bedroom to the kitchen downstairs and was cared for by other residents whilst the Police were sent for.

On the arrival of the Police, Yung Yap was removed to hospital. The Police then began a search of the area to trace See Lee who appeared to have gone to ground, hidden by his friends in the Chinese community.

Some hours later as a result of information given to them, Police Officers attended at Lime Street Railway Station, Liverpool, where they arrested See Lee who was attempting to escape by boarding a train to Glasgow.

He later told Police, he had intended going to Glasgow, and then onto Cardiff, both cities had large Chinese communities.

At the Police Station, See Lee told the Officers that Yung Yap was jealous of his relationship with Amy Yap Sing.

He went on to tell the police interviewing him that when he had arrived at Amy's room, Yung Yap was sitting on a chair and upon seeing See Lee, he had taken a revolver out of his pocket and pointed it at him. See Lee said he had taken the revolver off Yung Yap and shot him, otherwise Yung Yap would have shot him.

Later on he made a second statement to Police in which he said he had tried to take the pistol from Yung Yap, but hadn't succeeded. In the struggle the pistol had gone off, and Yung Yap had shot himself.

The Police in the meantime had interviewed Yung Yap who had told them See Lee had entered the room but never spoke. He simply shot me with a revolver. I don't know why he shot me, I have never had a quarrel with him.

Three days later having failed to recover from his injury, Yung Yap died from septic poison caused by the gun wound.

See Lee was now charged with murder, and later appeared before Liverpool Magistrates Court; he was remanded in custody.

On 12th March, 1909, the trial of See Lee took place at St Georges Hall, Liverpool. Lee pleaded not guilty to the charge of murder and was represented in court by Mr A.R. Kennedy, and Mr H Riley who was instructed on behalf of the Chinese Consul General. The Prosecution was conducted by Mr Rathbone and Mr Rees.

The Prosecution Barrister, Mr Rathbone outlined the case on behalf of the crown. He then read out a statement taken from the deceased man Yung Yap in which he described the incident which led to him losing his life.

Amy Yap Sing was closely cross examined by Mr Riley on behalf of the defendant regarding the shooting incident. She stated that she had never seen the revolver, but she had seen Yung Yap reel from the gunshot, he had then collapsed across her bed. She was then challenged that Yung Yap owned a revolver, but denied any knowledge of seeing either man with a gun.

Two members of the Chinese community were called by the prosecution to tell the court the deceased man Yung

Yap was a quiet and steady man. He was well known to them, and had never been seen with a gun.

The most damming piece of evidence against the defendant was given by Dr Simpson, of the Royal Southern Hospital, who told the court that from the route the bullet had taken in the body of the deceased, the revolver must have been pointed directly at the side of the deceased.

He went on to say it was impossible that Yung Yap could have shot himself with his right hand, and that it would have been extremely awkward to do it with his left hand.

When cross examined by Mr Riley, he did concede that it was possible the weapon may have gone off in a struggle whilst still in the deceased man's hand.

Lee See in giving his evidence maintained that it was Yung Yap who had the revolver, and it was during the struggle that the gun fired. He told the court that he had never owned a revolver, but he had seen the deceased with a revolver in one of the Chinese gambling houses.

During his closing speech, Mr Riley stated it would have been more likely that if See Lee had deliberately shot the man in a jealous rage, he would have stood gloating over the injured man, instead of slinking away like a frightened man.

The jury having listened to the evidence took just ten minutes to find See Lee guilty of the crime.

His Lordship after assuming the black cap proceeded to pass sentence of death upon the convicted man.

See Lee he said had been convicted on the clearest possible evidence, of the deliberate murder of a man who was said to have been his friend.

His Lordship could see no motive for the crime, but that of jealousy. He advised the prisoner to do his utmost to make his peace with the almighty.

He told him he must not entertain any hope that the sentence would not be carried out.

The accused man displayed not the slightest emotion upon hearing the sentence of death passed on him.

During his remand in Walton Prison, See Lee was visited by staff from the Chinese Consul who promised to pass on any messages to Lee's family back in China.

On 26th March, 1909, a letter was received by the Solicitor acting for See Lee stating that the Home Secretary could find no grounds for recommending a reprieve in the case of See Lee. The information was given to the condemned man the same day.

On Tuesday, 30th March, 1909 the execution of See Lee was carried out by Henry Albert Pierpoint who was assisted by his brother, Thomas William Pierpoint.

At the Coroners inquest held within the Prison later that morning, the Prison Governor John Dillion was able to tell the court that sentence of death had been carried out at 9 a.m. that morning. It was performed humanely and expeditiously, and in a skilful and decorous manner.

There was not the least hitch in the arrangement, and death was instantaneous.

The jury returned a verdict of death by lawful hanging.

# The Execution of Henry Thompson

Henry Thompson, 54 years, a Marine fireman by trade, lived with his wife Mary, 47 years in rented rooms in York Street, Liverpool.

The house itself was a large terraced building that had been divided into rooms, a Mr and Mrs Reynolds renting the remaining rooms.

Henry and Mary had been married for some eight years, their relationship from the start had been one of drink and violence. How the marriage had lasted no-one could tell, as there appeared to be no love between the couple.

Often in a drunken stupor, Henry would be violent towards his wife. The Police had been called to the premises on many occasions. Mary however would always refuse to make any complaint against her husband.

Mr and Mrs Reynolds who shared the house with the Thompsons tried to keep out of the way when both of them were rowing, but living very close to each other sometimes made this impossible. The sound of raised voices could be heard throughout the house.

On Saturday, 31st July, 1910 the couple were out earlier than usual, visiting the local drinking houses. Somehow during the evening, they had become separated, and Henry rather the worse for drink arrived home before Mary.

At 11.30 p.m. Mary arrived home to be greeted at the front door by Henry who was in a foul mood.

The Reynolds who had been having a quite evening at home, stopped talking and listened to the argument that was taking place on the doorstep between Henry and his wife.

Henry shouted at Mary "You can go where you have been all night, if you come into this house I will kill you stone dead. I have been near hung for somebody and I will be hung for you before long".

Mary however managed to get inside the house, and changed into her nightdress. She had hoped Henry would stop arguing and fall asleep.

The situation now took a turn for the worse, Henry started to threaten her. Fearing that Henry would harm her, she sought refuge with Mr and Mrs Reynolds. The couple seeing that Mary was terrified told her to hide at the side of their bed next to the wall.

Henry in the meantime had followed Mary into the room, and dragged her back by the neck. Mrs Reynolds protested and Henry threatened to throw her through the window for interfering.

Some minutes later Mary was heard to say "Harry don't choke me". Mrs Reynolds at this point went and banged on the Thompson's door, shouting for Henry to leave his wife alone.

Henry shouted back at her, "Mind your own business, we are going to bed" . Nothing more was heard from Mary or Henry and Mrs Reynolds went back to her room hoping the feuding couple had settled down for the night.

Some time later the Reynolds were awakened by banging on the floor. This noise was then followed by something being dragged across the floor in the Thompson's room.

At 12 noon the following day, Henry Thompson came into the shared kitchen and asked Mrs Reynolds for some water. Mrs Reynolds offered to take Mary some tea. Henry refused saying his wife had just finished her breakfast.

Later that day Henry called on Mrs Reynolds, and asked her to cook some meat as his wife was hungry.

Mrs Reynolds by now had become quite concerned for Mary's safety, and with another woman called at the Thompson's room. Henry in no uncertain terms told the women to go away, pushing them away from the door.

Thompson left the house for a short time and Mr Reynolds managed to gain access to the bedroom but he could find no sign of Mary.

On Monday, 2nd August, 1910, Mrs Reynolds waited for Henry Thompson to leave the house and then entered the Thompson's bedroom and discovered the body of Mary Thompson lying dead in the bed, a red handkerchief covered her face.

The Police were called to the scene and immediately began a search for Henry Thompson. He was arrested a short time later but became so violent that he was forcibly handcuffed, and remained so for some hours whilst in the Police station.

During his interview with the Police, he commented that he was "Fixed this time". He also added "The ...... thing was like a dummy in the bed beside me".

He appeared in the Magistrates Court on Tuesday, 3rd August, 1910, and was remanded in custody to appear before Liverpool Assizes Court.

On 16th October, 1910, Henry Thompson appeared before Mr Justice Avory at Liverpool Assizes Court. He pleaded not guilty to the offence of murdering his wife.

The trial lasted four hours, and the jury having retired for some twenty minutes returned with a guilty verdict.

The Clerk of the Court asked Thompson if he had anything

to say, why sentence of death should not be passed upon him. Thompson shouted back in a loud voice "No, go on with it, I don't care, I am not frightened of death".

His Lordship said the jury had done their duty, and it only remained for him to do his. He then passed sentence of death upon Thompson who shouted out "Amen".

Thompson was remanded to Walton Prison to await the sentence of the law to be carried out.

Whilst in Walton Prison, Thompson remained in a terrible sore mood, it was only in his last days that his mood changed, and he spent most of his time with the Roman Catholic Chaplain of the Prison, Father Browne.

On Monday, 21st November, 1910 word was received at the Prison that the Home Secretary had decided he could not interfere in the sentence that had been passed down by the court.

The information was conveyed to Thompson who accepted the decision with a shake of the head.

On Tuesday, 22nd, November, 1910, Henry Thompson was up and about the condemned cell at an early hour and attended mass in the prison chapel.

Upon returning to his cell he refused breakfast, waiting for Father Browne to join him. Both men then sat on Thompson's bed, Father Browne leading Thompson in prayer.

The Prison Officers who had been watching over Thompson sat nearby, knowing the time of execution was fast approaching.

The morning outside was bitterly cold with a heavy frost lying on the ground. A crowd of four hundred people had gathered outside and members of the Liverpool branch for the abolition of capital punishment paraded up and down outside the prison carrying placards.

At 8.55 a.m. John Ellis the executioner appeared at the condemned cell, in the room next door, he strapped Thompson's arm's to his side. He then took his place in the procession that made its way towards the execution chamber.

Thompson walked at a steady pace, he entered the execution chamber, and walked up to the gallows. John Ellis completed strapping Thomson, and pulled the death mask over his head. The noose was placed around his neck and, after a signal from the Prison Governor, John Ellis pulled the trap door lever sending Henry Thompson to his death.

# The Execution of Thomas Seymour

The story of the crime Thomas Seymour was executed for, was a callous act that shocked the people of Liverpool.

The crime was so brutal, people who knew Thomas Seymour refused to believe he was capable of such a murderous act.

Thomas Seymour, 65 years, had been a seafaring man most of his working life. He had saved enough money during his employment which would carry him through his retirement years, or so he thought.

Seymour was not known to be a heavy drinker whilst at sea, but on returning to dry land, he could drink with the best of them. He was a quiet, but popular man with a lot of friends. Being the man he was, he would often stand his friends a round of drinks.

The money he had saved up whilst at sea, was slowly but surely ebbing away.

Since settling down, he had lived the life of a single man, but lately he had become involved with a lady who was a distant cousin. Both of them seemed to get on well together at first, the relationship grew and after a while the couple married, and lived at Breckfield Place, Everton.

The lady prior to marrying had been left a sum of money. Seymour was aware of this fact, whether this persuaded him to get married is something that is not known.

The marriage was not a happy one, Mrs Seymour was addicted to drink, and Thomas himself was alcoholic.

The murder itself was discovered by a female relative of Mrs Seymour who had called to speak to her. Upon being admitted to the house by Thomas Seymour, she was shocked to find Mrs Seymour lying dead in a corner of the room. She immediately left the house and went in search of a policeman.

Thomas Seymour now realizing the gravity of the situation, went into Breckfield Place and upon seeing a Police Constable went up to the Officer and told him he had just killed his wife.

The Police Officer believed Seymour was drunk, but on his insistence accompanied him back to his house. Upon entering the premises he found Mrs Seymour lying dead with a dreadful head wound, hot ashes were scattered over the poor woman's body.

Seymour was arrested and taken to the Police Station, and made a full confession to the murder. He had hit his wife over the head with a blunt instrument fracturing her skull. He had then thrown ashes over her body to soak up the blood that had flowed from the dreadful wound.

He appeared at the Magistrates Court the following day and was remanded in custody to Walton Prison.

Whilst at the Prison, he was kept under observation by Dr Prior, the Medical Officer buthe displayed no signs of being insane.

He later appeared before Mr Justice Avory, at Liverpool Spring Assizes Court, and pleaded guilty to the charge.

He confessed his crime with such frankness, his Lordship put the hearing back to enable Seymour to consult with his barrister in view of the crime carrying a mandatory death sentence.

Upon returning to court Seymour again pleaded guilty to the crime, leaving Mr Justice Avory to do nothing other than pass sentence of death.

Thomas Seymour was conveyed back to Walton Prison, this time he was placed in the condemned cell to await his fate.

Whilst under sentence of death, Seymour was reported to be acting with that strange indifference which he had shown throughout his trial.

He however gave no trouble to the Prison Officers who had been assigned to watch over him during his last days.

Information was given to the Home Secretary in an appeal for a reprieve, that on the morning of the murder, he had visited the Sailors and Fireman's Union Office, and paid his subscription, so that if anything went wrong with him, his " Widow " might get something.

The Home Secretary after reviewing the facts of the case, declined to interfere with the sentence of the court.

At 8 a.m. on Tuesday, 9th, May, 1911, a crowd of two hundred people gathered outside the Prison, the weather was mild, the sun was attempting to break though the light clouds that hung over the city.

At 8.45 a.m. the Prison clock began a steady and monotonous chime, the crowd standing outside the Prison went quiet, knowing that the other side of the grim walls Thomas Seymour was about to make his last journey.

The execution was carried out without any hitch whatsoever. Thomas Seymour offered no resistance, and submitted quietly to the executioner.

Death had been instantaneous, the Coroners jury later returning a verdict of death by hanging.

The executioner was John Ellis, assisted by Thomas Pierpoint.

The following instructions were given to Prisons in which executions were carried out.

# INSTRUCTIONS TO BE OBSERVED IN BURYING THE BODIES OF EXECUTED PRISONERS.

1.  All the clothing with the exception of the shirt or similar garment will be removed from the body which will be placed in a coffin made of half inch wood, deal or pine.

2.  The sides and ends of the coffin will be perforated with large holes.

3.  Lime will not be used.

4.  The original size of the plot of ground will be 9ft. By 4ft, and the grave will be from 8 to 10ft in depth.

5.  When the coffin has been covered with 1 foot of earth, charcoal to the depth of three inches will be thrown onto the grave, which will then be filled in. The top coffin will not be less than 4 feet below the ground surface.

6.  Arrangements will be made for the grave sites to be re-used in sequence, in such wise that no grave will be used over again until seven years have elapsed. When a grave is re-opened the charcoal and the foot of earth above the last coffin will not be disturbed.

7.  A register of graves will be kept, containing the name of each convict buried, the date of the burial, the site of the grave, and the position of the coffin in the grave.

This is the first book in a series of three.  Look out for parts two and three coming shortly.